Net That Job

Using the World Wide Web to develop your career and find work

Irene Krechowiecka

KOGAN PAGE

YOURS TO HAVE AND TO HOLD
BUT NOT TO COPY

First published in 1998

Apart from any fair dealing for the purposes of research or private study, or criticism or review, as permitted under the Copyright, Designs and Patents Act 1988, this publication may only be reproduced, stored or transmitted, in any form or by any means, with the prior permission in writing of the publishers, or in the case of reprographic reproduction in accordance with the terms and licences issued by the CLA. Enquiries concerning reproduction outside those terms should be sent to the publishers at the undermentioned address:

Kogan Page Limited
120 Pentonville Road
London N1 9JN

© Irene Krechowiecka 1998

The right of Irene Krechowiecka to be identified as author of this work has been asserted by her in accordance with the Copyright, Designs and Patents Act 1988.

British Library Cataloguing in Publication Data

A CIP record for this book is available from the British Library.

ISBN 0 7494 2574 1

Typeset by JS Typesetting, Wellingborough, Northants.
Printed in England by Biddles Ltd, Guildford and King's Lynn.

To Christopher and Rob, who know more about computers than I ever will. Thanks for filling in the gaps.

Contents

Contents

Acknowledgements

I would like to thank all the people who took the time to talk and write to me about their use of the Web and their vision of its future. Particular thanks go to Pete Erguano for giving me the initial impetus, Marcus Offer for his information on European sites, Becky Griffiths at Recruitnet, the BBC, GTI, Intel, Boeing, Cool Works, Shell International, The Monster Board and KPMG.

While every effort has been made to check the accuracy of the information included, I would be happy to receive e-mails with suggestions, corrections and updates at:

irene.k@unforgettable.com

Introduction

Knowledge is of two kinds. We know a subject ourselves or we know where we can find information upon it.

Samuel Johnson

This book will help you find a job using the World Wide Web. It looks at how this incredible resource can be harnessed to choose or develop your career and find a job you will enjoy getting up for. It is a guide for those who, like me, aren't computer experts and don't have unlimited time and money to spend on exploring the Internet. It will show you how to get the maximum benefit from it for minimum effort and expense.

Effective job hunting and career development require access to accurate, relevant and up-to-date information. Computer-based information is increasingly used in the guidance and job-seeking process because computers are unsurpassable in their ability to store, process and update information. Many of the organizations that create and collect careers information want to share it with any interested individual. The Internet enables them to do this on a huge scale. With access to it you can select from some of the best information, advice and help available and find thousands of current vacancies anywhere in the world. If you know where to look, it will be less time-consuming and more productive than any other method. *Net That Job* identifies what you need to look for, as well as how and where to look. It explains and examines the contribution Web-based information can make to career planning and job hunting, listing and describing sites relevant to each stage of the process.

If you have used Windows software but are not familiar with Internet use, Appendix A will help you to get started. Tips on economic and effective use of the Internet and accessing it – even if you don't have a computer – are in Appendix B.

The unlimited information available on the Internet can bring problems sooner than solutions. Some of the information is excellent, some is mediocre, some is positively harmful. This book will help you evaluate the quality of careers information and discriminate between the worthwhile and the worthless.

The Internet is a fluid medium: Netscape describe it as 'an untamed frontier'. Because its content is constantly changing, it's not possible, or even desirable, to provide a comprehensive guide. Users need techniques that will help them to construct their own routes through to where they want to be. This book concentrates on techniques rather than technicalities. Technicalities change, addresses change, sites come and go, but what you learn here should be adaptable to change.

The advice given and techniques described applied before the Internet existed, and will continue to apply in the future. They concentrate on human communication and interaction, which makes use of all the tools available. Using the World Wide Web as part of your career development and job hunting is a way of demonstrating that you have abilities, qualities and attitudes that employers are looking for. It provides a concrete example of your being able to use the communications technology of the future.

1
The Web

This chapter explains the contribution the World Wide Web can make to job hunting. It also examines and addresses the sorts of concerns many of us have about its use.

- The Internet
- The World Wide Web
- Changes in the world of work
- Common fears about using the Internet – your questions answered

THE INTERNET

The Internet consists of millions of computers across the world linked by the telephone network. It is a system for storing and moving information around. No one controls the Internet; people just participate in it by making information available and using it in various ways. There is no censorship and no enforceable set of standards governing its content. It reflects all that's good and bad in the world in an unfiltered way. The US Supreme Court recently ruled against Internet censorship; 'Content on the Internet is as diverse as human thought', said Justice Paul Stevens, 'the interest in encouraging freedom of expression in a democratic society outweighs any theoretical but unproven benefit of censorship'.

These connected computers allow people to communicate and share information in a new way. With an Internet connection, your home computer can be linked to much more powerful machines, which in turn provide you with a link to everyone else with an Internet connection. Information stored anywhere in the world can be made available to anyone who wants it.

No one knows how big the Internet is. In mid 1997 it was estimated to have 60 million users worldwide and be growing at 2 per cent a week. An NOP poll in December 1996 estimated that 10 per cent of the adult population in the UK (4.6 million people) were using it. The most visually attractive part of the Internet is the World Wide Web, and this is what many people think of as the Internet. It is often referred to as 'the Web', WWW or W3.

THE WORLD WIDE WEB

The Web is like a glossy multimedia magazine that allows you to access information from all over the world on every subject. That information is usually presented in an attractive way and includes links to related information. This gives it a web-like structure; following one connection leads to others, which in turn link to related information. It means that you can look at things in greater depth and make connections you might not otherwise have thought of. It can also mean that you end up going round in circles, feeling trapped and frustrated. In theory you can find information on everything you would ever want, and then some more, with the click of a mouse. In practice you need to spend a little time developing efficient search techniques and a basic understanding of what is happening in order to utilize the tremendous potential it offers.

Anyone can set up a web site that is then accessible to everyone else. Although there is little contentious information related to careers guidance and job hunting, inaccurate or misleading information is worse than no information at all. Many of the sources of careers and vacancy information on the Web come from organizations that would only produce quality material, whatever medium they were using. However, it is up to the user to evaluate the standard and usefulness of what they look at. Guidelines on how to do this are given in Chapter 3.

As a user wanting to retrieve information from the Web, there is very little you need to know about computers. Basic keyboarding skills are enough to enable you to use it smoothly. The screens you work with are similar to those on word processors. What you do need to learn, is how to search for the information you want effectively and avoid being swamped by irrelevant material. It's like a huge encyclopaedia, with many different contents and index pages that can be searched in different ways. Details of how to connect to the Internet and find your way around the WWW are contained in Appendix A.

Most Internet connections give you access to news groups, e-mail, file transfer protocol, and Internet relay chat as well as to the Web. This book concentrates on the WWW, but the other areas are described briefly in relation to job hunting.

CHANGES IN THE WORLD OF WORK

The world of work constantly changes to reflect a changing world. Predictions about how things will alter in the future are nearly always wrong. It's more useful to look at what is happening now, and what implications current changes have for jobseekers.

- Unskilled jobs are decreasing, but jobs at all levels increasingly require some computer literacy.
- Employers look for evidence of being able to adapt to change and a willingness to understand and use new technologies.
- People are more likely to change jobs and career areas. The job for life is a rarity.
- There is a trend towards globalization of the labour market.
- Technological developments mean that a wider range of work can be done from 'remote' locations. This removes some previous geographical restrictions, and increases the need for computer competency.

The continuing development of new communication and information technologies has contributed significantly to alterations in employment patterns. Changes in the labour market mean that jobseekers have to acquire skills that show they are aware of these developments and can adapt to the changes they cause.

INTERNET FEARS – YOUR QUESTIONS ANSWERED

The growth and use of the Internet generates much discussion. Telephones and computers already have a significant influence on our daily lives, often not perceived by us, and on their own no longer arouse much interest or controversy. By combining these two technologies, the Internet has created a new culture with its own language and conventions, and has led to new concerns about how it will affect our lives. Some of the adverse publicity it receives serves to put many people off finding out more. A network of computers, in itself, cannot be good or evil – it simply transmits the ideas of others. The use to which it is put, however, depends on the individuals who use it.

For those who have read or heard about the Internet rather than used it, it's easy to find reasons for not becoming involved.

'I don't like computers or the people who use them – they appear obsessed with them.'

Have you given computers a chance? Don't write off the possibility of a satisfying, productive and non-obsessive relationship with one until you do! Let a friend show you, or join a class. There are increasing numbers of information technology (IT) training opportunities, many of them free. For details of UK provision and contacts see Appendix B.

Most jobs, regardless of level or occupational sector, require some familiarity with IT. Lack of it, or reluctance to acquire it, is increasingly likely to prevent you from getting a job. Presently, one in four UK companies is connected to the Internet and one in six has a web site! That number is expected to increase significantly.

'Careers guidance is a personal thing, how can a computer have anything to offer me?'

Guidance needs to be supported by accurate information. Computerized packages that can store and process information related to career choice are widely used and make a valuable contribution to many of the activities of guidance. The Web provides you with a link to this resource and to people who can help you benefit from it. However, using the Web should only form a part of the careers guidance and job-seeking process. It should enhance, not replace, other means of communication and research.

'I can't afford to buy a computer and all the other expensive hardware and software you need for an Internet connection.'

It's not essential to have your own computer. There is an ever-increasing number of places that offer free or cheap access to the Internet (see Appendix B).

'There's so much jargon associated with it, I don't think I could ever understand it.'

Anything new needs new words to describe it. Words and phrases that are associated with Internet use are explained simply in the Glossary at the end of the book.

'It's an ever-changing medium, anything you learn is out of date before you can put it to use.'

It does change quickly, that's one of the advantages it has over other media. At its best this means information is regularly updated. The structure of the Web is such that it enables users and providers to communicate details of changes easily. Some sites incorporate a facility to notify you of changes or leave a message to tell you where they have moved to (see Figure 1.1). There is even a company offering a free service that informs you when a web site address changes.

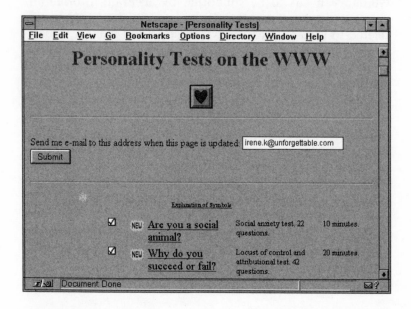

Figure 1.1 Many Web sites include a facility that keeps you informed of significant changes.

See under URL minders, Sites worth seeing, at the end of Appendix B for details of how to use this for pages of your choice.

'I've heard that people can become addicted to the Internet.'

True. The aim of this book is to help you use the enormous potential it has without becoming addicted, distracted or bankrupt!

'All the information on the WWW is somewhere else too, so why bother?'

Because it's one of the easiest ways to find and access information. It's always open and available. For job vacancies it should
be more up to date than any paper publications. You can often
see a post advertised, get a detailed job description, company
information and application form well before the vacancy
appears in print. The way information is presented on the Web
enables you to make links you may not have otherwise thought
of. This should give greater depth and breadth to your research.

'People say it takes ages to get anywhere and that WWW stands for World Wide Wait!'

It can take a long time to access some pages, while others appear
almost instantaneously. The time it takes to transfer information depends on a number of factors that are explained in
Appendix B, where you will also find techniques and suggestions for optimizing the speed at which you receive information.

'It's a good way of infecting your computer with viruses!'

True, that's why it's important to install an up-to-date virus
check program. There are many such available as free downloads. Be sure to install one before you download any of the
other free or priced software you'll be tempted by.

'There's too much information there, it will take so much time to find anything worth-while that it will slow down the process of job hunting.'

True, if you let it. This book aims to help you avoid that. Like
any web, it is a beguiling, attractive creation that it's all too
easy to get trapped in. You need to work out what you want

from it and then conduct focused searches. All the techniques for doing that are given in the following chapters.

'A lot of the information is of poor quality – it's too unregulated to be of real use.'

The WWW is unregulated. It works like a cooperative rather than a corporation. That doesn't necessarily mean that all the information is poor. As with all sources of information, there is a great variety in the quality of what is produced. You do need to be discriminating and assess the nature and quality of what you're looking at. This is a skill you will need in a whole range of employment and job seeking situations too! Guidelines on how to assess the quality of information are to be found in Chapter 3.

'Some of the best sites are protected by passwords and you need to subscribe before you can access them.'

All the sites referred to in this book have free access. Many sites – such as recruitment agencies, newspaper recruitment sites, e-mail sites – do issue you with a personal password, but no cost is involved. They do it to make sure only you can access any personal information submitted.

'A lot of sites are just advertising things they want you to buy. They give a free trial period and then you're hooked.'

Some do this, but the chance to evaluate software, information, even personal counselling services, is a bonus. Try before you buy. This is particularly useful in relation to Internet service providers (see Appendix B). The bulk of information and many of the services on the WWW are free. This may change, but, at present, a spirit of generosity and cooperation still prevails. If the service or information you are looking for has a price, check if there is something similar available for free and see how it compares.

'It's too distracting, you'll spend time looking at interesting links and never get round to finding a job.'

... or writing a book! The Web's potential for distraction is the biggest problem and the biggest attraction. Having been thoroughly distracted, I've managed to devise search and browsing techniques that help minimize temptation. However, sometimes even distractions can prove useful.

'All the jobs advertised on the Internet are for graduates in IT, and they're mainly in the USA.'

That was the case a few years ago. It is now possible to find jobs in all occupational sectors, at all levels, in most countries. There are vacancies for gardeners and geologists, cleaners and chief executives, sports reporters and spies!

'It's got information on it that I wouldn't want my children to see.'

The software you get from an Internet service provider can include programs that will allow you to control access to certain sites. Your provider will be able to advise you on this.

'It sounds good value, but the cost of phone calls and other fees could really add up.'

It does. Being aware of the cost is one way of ensuring that you conduct short, focused searches and don't allow yourself to become distracted. If used in this way, it can work out cheaper than obtaining the same information by more traditional means. See under Cheap Cuts in Appendix B for ideas on how to use the Web in the most economical way.

`Nobody gives anything away for free – what's the catch, what's in it for them?'

Different things for different people/organizations. Everybody gains, but not necessarily financially. Employers and employment agencies use the WWW to advertise their products and services, make people aware of their culture and values and reach a wider population of potential employees. Academic and professional institutions use it to spread knowledge and good practice. Other organizations and individuals may state their aims. It's worth checking what those are. For example, I would feel uneasy about doing a personality test supplied by a religious cult, but not about one offered by an academic institution. Look at sites critically, work out what their purpose is before devoting time to exploring them.

`It's all a bit too fast. Letters take time to get there, and that gives me a breathing space to reflect on what I've done, rather than having to react immediately.'

Speed has its advantages, particularly if you are an employer wanting to fill a post quickly. Your reflection should have been done at an earlier stage. Before applying for a job, you should spend time preparing for the consequences of that application. Thorough self-assessment is essential for effective job hunting. How to use the Web to do this is dealt with in Chapter 2.

`It makes me uneasy to think that anyone could access personal information about me. It doesn't seem very secure.'

There have been problems relating to security of information and worries over making financial details available. Systems for secure transactions on the Web are improving. In relation to personal information, such as details on a CV, you can decide how many people see it by choosing where you send it (see under Employment Agencies, Chapter 4). Information transmitted electronically can, in theory, be read by anyone unless it is encrypted. It is like sending a postcard rather than a sealed letter. If this worries you, don't send personal information from insecure sites. There is usually a facility in your browser software to indicate the status of the site you are using. With Netscape, for example you will see a key symbol at the bottom of each Web page. If this is unbroken it means that information sent to and from that site is secure, if it's broken it means it's not. The page shown in Figure 1.1 (page 8) is not secure.

'I'm convinced! I'll never lick a stamp, make a phone call or visit a library or careers office again.'

A monumental mistake. The WWW is one medium, one source of information among many. You need to integrate it with other forms of communication. It is not always the best or most appropriate method. You have to exercise judgement and discrimination. Always consider if there is an alternative way of accessing information or communicating and whether Internet use has any advantage over more traditional means. Employers don't want people who can only communicate or conduct research electronically. They generally want people who can relate to others by a variety of means and in a variety of situations. It's nice to get real letters, libraries have good books (and cheap Internet access) and careers advisers are good to talk to!

Self-assessment

This chapter explains the uses and benefits of tests commonly used for employment-related assessment and recruitment. It shows how material freely available on the WWW can be used for personal self-assessment and as a preparation for assessments by employers.

- The need for self-assessment
- Using the Web for self-assessment
- Self-assessment tools
- Regulation of test use
- Practice tests
- Other Web resources
- Sites worth seeing
- Summary

THE NEED FOR SELF-ASSESSMENT

Think about it this way – if you are no good at maths you won't enjoy being a mathematician. Sounds simple, doesn't it? But you'd be surprised how many people are working in jobs they simply hate because they didn't go in for a bit of self-analysis before taking them on.

GTI web-site

Work makes up a large part of most people's lives. Being unhappy at work is destructive; finding something that matches your personality and skills is motivating, enjoyable and energizing. The first stage in making an informed decision about career choice, change and development is self-assessment. You need to know what you're good at, what you like and dislike, what sort of lifestyle you want, what you expect from, and want to give to, your employer.

Going through a thorough process of self-assessment gives you the information you need to identify career areas that are worth an investment of your time and effort. It should also enable you to see if your aims are realistic. If you are confident about your suitability for a particular career area, it will be much easier to convince a potential employer of the same. The information you gain about yourself gives you the basic material for your application forms and interviews. It helps you to articulate your strengths, abilities and qualities. This is something you will repeatedly be asked to do when applying for jobs. If you don't know what your good points are, it will be difficult to convince an employer that you have any.

Applying for jobs means subjecting yourself to scrutiny by others, who will measure you against their own predetermined standards. Assessing yourself first and seeing what they are likely to find can give you confidence when submitting yourself to this potentially stressful and threatening process. It can also help you avoid applying for jobs that are not right for you.

Employers aren't secretive about their selection criteria: it's in everyone's interest that unsuitable applications should be avoided. They are looking for evidence that the applicant has considered the requirements of the post in relation to their capabilities and aspirations and found that they are a close match. In many cases, their web sites offer information that can be treated as an extended self-assessment exercise, enabling potential applicants to see how well they could meet the needs of that company. The following is an extract from Shell International's web site:

So. How can we help you?
Maybe that's not how you would expect a corporate recruitment site to begin. Traditionally, we should start by declaring our wish to recruit high-calibre people to join uniquely rewarding,

demanding, diverse and enjoyable careers with our leading global organization . . . It's not just about being academically excellent – though we want that, too – we seek a diverse range of people who are all-round human beings; high achievers in life as well as in college, who will bring with them the combination of resourcefulness, intelligence and personality we need to realize our exciting ambitions for the future . . . This site outlines who we are and what we seek . . . Most importantly, this site will help you learn about yourself. Are you right for us? Have you the right qualifications and qualities? What can you achieve? What can we do to help you?

Looking at yourself objectively, deciding on priorities and seeing yourself as others do is not an easy thing to achieve. Most people feel quite comfortable undertaking a light-hearted quiz in a magazine that claims to shed light on their personality, but less so when undertaking a more scientifically devised test, particularly if the results contribute towards a decision on their suitability for a job or promotion. Tests of various types are used by employers for this purpose. Such tests also have value for individuals wishing to measure their skills, aptitudes and preferences in a detached and methodical way.

USING THE WEB FOR SELF-ASSESSMENT

Tests, questionnaires and other assessment exercises require information to be processed and so make good use of computer technology. The Web enables access to a range of computerized assessment programs and demolishes some of the barriers that have prevented anybody and everybody accessing such material. At the same time, it removes some of the safeguards that previously ensured it was used appropriately. The user of freely available IQ, aptitude and personality tests needs a basic understanding of their function, potential benefits and limitations in order to be able to select what is most appropriate.

There are numerous sites on the Web that can offer information on, and tools for, self-assessment. These consist of:

● sites that give background information and general guidance on how to prepare for tests;

- sites offering free access to a range of self-assessment tools;
- news groups where you can communicate with others who've been through the experience (see Figure 2.1);
- occupational psychologists and others offering a testing, scoring and interpretation service for a fee;
- details of tests held in academic libraries that are often available for student research purposes;
- reviews of specific tests and articles about the subject of psychometric testing in general.

Where access to tests is unregulated, it is important to be able to differentiate a useful tool from a useless or even harmful one. The following sections will help you understand the uses of different types of tests and inventories and give you a framework for evaluating material that is available on the Web.

SELF-ASSESSMENT TOOLS

Interest inventories

These are commonly used as a starting point in careers guidance. They are a tool that helps the individual think systematically about their interests and preferences, relating these to occupational areas or specific jobs. Interest inventories form a useful basis for discussion and can help broaden ideas and options or serve to confirm the suitability of existing ideas. They are not tests. They do not have right or wrong answers and they do not claim to predict success. They are looking at likes and dislikes, not abilities.

In some cases, an individual's skills and abilities match their preferences. People often like doing what they know they are good at, but not always. You can like music, but be hopeless at performing it, you can enjoy communicating with people, but they may not enjoy listening to you. An interest inventory produces a snapshot of how you feel at one particular time. Likes and dislikes, interests and preferences can and do change. The results of an interest inventory should therefore be treated as if they have a 'best before date' of no more than a year!

Interest inventories are widely available in careers centres, schools, colleges and universities in both paper and computerized form. They are informative, fun to do and have been selected for their relevance to local users. If you have access to them in this way, you will probably have the opportunity to discuss the results with an adviser, which gives added value to the exercise. If not, you can find a large number of sites offering something similar on the Web. A selection of sites is given at the end of this chapter and many more can be found using a search engine. You need to be aware of the limitations of such exercises and remember that the results are in the nature of suggestions to be explored and discussed, rather than a prescription for the future. They have to be balanced by other factors.

When evaluating the potential usefulness of a Web-based interest inventory, look for the following.

- **Where it originates.** Many are from careers guidance providers, schools and universities and are therefore likely to have been tried, tested and found to be worth while. The country of origin can also be significant. As the Web is a global medium, inventories can originate in different countries. A questionnaire that comes from the USA may refer you to job matches that are not widely available in the UK or Sweden, for example. In most cases, however, the occupational areas and jobs suggested are fairly international.

- **Information about the inventory.** How large a bank of occupations does it have to compare your answers to? When was it last updated? Are data available on its development and suggested use?

- **Consider how relevant the questions seem to your situation.** There is no point answering a whole lot of questions that bear no relation to your personal circumstances and needs.

Sites that are free do not usually offer further guidance or interpretation of results. It is always useful to discuss findings from interest inventories with someone trained in their interpretation, and this may be available at no charge at a local college or careers centre.

Psychometric tests

An interest inventory is a good starting point, but it's only one small piece in the complicated jigsaw that makes up the 'all round human being' that Shell and other employers are looking for. As well as having different likes and dislikes, individuals have different aptitudes and skills, they vary in their motivation and values and have different personalities that affect the way they relate to people and situations.

When you apply for a job, employers assume that you are doing so because your interests are matched by the content of that post. Their task is to evaluate your abilities, aptitudes and personality. Psychometric testing is one commonly used tool in this process. Its use is a widespread and sometimes controversial feature of selection for a range of jobs at all levels. It can also contribute significantly to an individual's self-assessment if used and interpreted appropriately.

Psychometric tests are ones that have been scientifically constructed and researched. They are administered and scored in a predetermined and consistent manner. The raw scores are referenced to a benchmark, which is usually sets of average scores for particular groups or a specific criterion of performance or aptitude. They are accompanied by a manual or supporting data that explain the theory and research behind the test and detail the uses and clients for whom it is appropriate. Particularly important is the information relating to reliability, validity and norms.

Reliability and validity

Reliability relates to the consistency of scores obtained in a test. Will the same person get roughly the same score each time they do the test? If not, then it's not a reliable test.

Validity data indicate how suitable a test is for measuring whatever it's meant to measure. A tape measure is not a valid tool for measuring weight.

In order to be of value in assessment, a test must be both valid and reliable. If it's not reliable it can't be valid, but being reliable does not guarantee validity. It's possible to be reliably bad. For example, a darts player who gets darts in all over the board is not reliable and not valid. One who consistently hits the light above the board is reliable but not valid. One who gets a bull's eye every time is both reliable and valid. Reputable psychometric tests therefore undergo trials and are tested for their validity and reliability. The data are made available to users to enable them to choose the most appropriate test for their situation.

Norms

Norms are data about how particular groups of people scored in the test. Each group is usually measured against its norm. The average school-leaver, for example, will not perform in the same way as the average postgraduate student, and it would be wrong to compare them. For a test to be meaningful, the norm group you are measuring yourself against should be at the right level. It should also relate to a category relevant to you. If you're a college student on a care course wanting to prepare for a test to enter nurse training, there's no point in doing a test of spatial ability designed for the selection of applicants for electrical engineering apprenticeships. Some tests have different norms for males and females, too, which reflect the fact that they have different strengths and aptitudes. The size of the norm group is important; the larger it is, the more representative and reliable it is likely to be.

Psychometric testing and job selection

The value of psychometric tests as a selection tool is often questioned. On the positive side, they can provide an objective assessment of an individual's capabilities and personality. Tests contribute towards creating an accurate picture if used correctly and in conjunction with other methods. This can work in your favour if your qualifications do not accurately reflect your abilities. Coopers & Lybrand, for example, use numerical or verbal reasoning tests 'if your academic record does not allow us to make a comprehensive assessment of your ability'.

Psychometric testing has not always been used wisely or well, and this has led to bad publicity. However, if the company you are applying to uses tests as part of its selection procedure, you are not really in a position to question their rationale for doing so. The only sensible thing to do is prepare for them, by understanding their purpose and working through practice material. This will increase your speed and confidence, enabling you to perform to the best of your ability in the real situation.

Types of psychometric tests

Psychometric tests commonly used by employers divide into three main categories:

- tests of personality
- tests of general intelligence
- tests of aptitudes.

Many employers use a combination of these to select employees.

Personality tests
These are used by employers to select individuals whose characteristics match their requirements. Skills tested include motivation, social skills, ability to work as part of a team, determination and adaptability. Different jobs require different personality profiles. Tests used are extremely sophisticated and incorporate checks to detect inconsistencies that show if you are trying to answer questions in a way that you think will please the employer. The value of doing such a test for yourself is that it will help you identify areas of work suited to your temperament.

IQ tests
Such tests are often used to help determine intellectual capacity and ability to cope with further training or education. Completing such a test for yourself will show how you compare to the general population and give an indication of the likely level of intellectual challenge you will comfortably cope with. If, for example, you left school with no qualifications, but feel that that does not accurately reflect your abilities, a high score in

an IQ test could give you the confidence to return to education. Some educational institutions use such tests to help mature students decide on an appropriate level of study.

Aptitude tests

These are skill specific. Those most commonly used test verbal, numerical and spatial reasoning. Employers often use these to pre-select candidates for interview. The norm group you are measured against is people successfully doing the job you are applying for. These tests require speed and accuracy, both of which can be enhanced by practice.

REGULATION OF TEST USE

Psychometric tests are not freely available to the general public. In order to purchase genuine tests, the buyer has to prove that they have undergone relevant training in their administration, scoring and interpretation. They also have to give an under-taking that the material will be kept in a secure place, as the value of the tests would be undermined if their actual contents were generally available. The Web is not a secure place, nor could material freely available on it be administered in a consistent manner. The tests available on it are therefore psychometric-type tests rather than actual tests used by employers and others. This does not mean that they have no value as a self-assessment tool, as many are similar to the real thing. Indeed, they have a real contribution to make towards helping you assess your strengths and weaknesses and preparing for taking actual tests. To their credit, most sites offering free tests give explanations of what they are, and what they can help with. Some highlight the fact that they are not 'real' tests. Obviously light-hearted ones include the personality tests based on your choice of lipstick or underwear. Others, such as the Keirsey Temperament Sorter (see under Sites Offering Free Access To Self-assessment Tools in the Sites Worth Seeing section at the end of this chapter for the address), are well-researched and widely used.

PRACTICE TESTS

The prospect of undergoing any sort of test makes most people nervous. Although you cannot change your IQ or aptitudes significantly by practising, if you are more confident about your ability to cope with a test, you will work quickly and accurately. Aptitude tests are usually timed, so speed is important, and this can be improved by practice. There is also a value in identifying areas of weakness. If the results of a numerical aptitude test show that you have forgotten your multiplication tables, then you can do something about it before sitting an employer's test. If any test gives you just a result and no commentary or interpretation, then it is not particularly worth while. The interpretation should enable you to understand what your score means, how your performance compares with that of others and who you're being compared with. If you're uncertain about why an organization is offering tests for free on the Web, you'll usually find that a section on their site invites feedback and comment. E-mail them with a query about the tests they offer. You could even ask questions about validity and reliability!

If you want to try a 'real' test, there is no shortage of companies and organizations offering the opportunity at a range of prices. If you choose to use one of these, find out which tests they are offering and information on their normal use. Ask about reliability, validity and the norm groups used for scoring and only do tests that apply to your situation. A reputable company should check this with you, as inappropriate tests can do more harm than good. The costs of such services vary enormously, so shop around. Check what feedback is given and whether this is included in the price of the test.

For both free and priced tests, you can look at assessments of their value by reading test reviews held in academic libraries, which are widely available on the Web. These can be located by entering the test name as your search criterion in a search engine or metacrawler. Employers usually give applicants details of which tests they will use and details of how to prepare for them. Again, use a search engine to find background material and enhance your preparation.

OTHER WEB RESOURCES

News and chat groups

The Web offers access to news and chat groups where you can communicate with others who have experienced the testing part of a company's recruitment procedure. Some companies – Shell International, for example (see Figure 2.1) – offer a facility for prospective applicants to discuss recruitment queries with current employees.

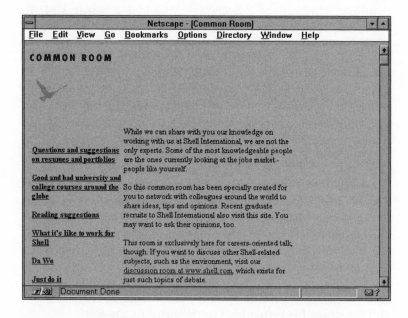

Figure 2.1 Shell International's Common Room is dedicated to careers and recruitment related queries. You can participate in existing discussions or start a new one.

Other providers of careers-related news and chat groups include employment agencies, such as The Monster Board, and general guidance sites, such as Gradunet. To find independent news groups that deal with these issues, use a search engine such as Deja News.

While the information gained in this way can be helpful, it should be treated with some caution. Other people's experiences are never going to be the same as your own. There is a very real danger in letting anecdotal evidence affect your performance in tests or other assessments. Candidates who feel they know what they're doing, as a result of first- or second-hand experience, often perform poorly. A little humility does no harm. What creates a negative impression is the attitude 'I know what they're after and I can outsmart them'. This is not to say that you shouldn't prepare as thoroughly as you can. Gaining knowledge from the experience of others can be valuable if used in conjunction with more objective sources of information, such as the graduate careers information sites listed at the end of this chapter. They have based their advice on the experiences of large numbers of students and from their contacts with recruiting employers – on fact rather than anecdote.

Help from employers' web sites

Tests, psychometric or otherwise, are not the only way to assess yourself. The web sites of many employers offer other facilities to help you decide whether or not you are suitable for them (see Figure 2.2).

Here an employer has made the links for you and led you by the hand, looking at the company, the job, their requirements and expectations. Different employers present information in different ways. Often it is up to you to look through the information provided and devise your own questions to see if you match their requirements. Doing this also provides the basic material you need to complete a focused and targeted application. Your preparation will be evident at interview.

Many employers use personal profiles as a way of showing the diversity of those likely to fit in to their environment and flourish in their organization. This is particularly true of occupations that have previously suffered from being stereotyped as dull. The web sites of many large accountancy companies, for example, are worth a visit if you still think that accountants just sit and look at numbers all day.

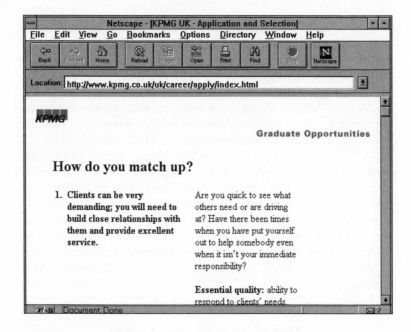

Figure 2.2 KPMG's web site features a self-assessment exercise tailored to the company's needs.

Profiles of successful and happy employees are carefully chosen to portray an image the employer wants to promote and give valuable clues to potential applicants (see Figure 2.3). What an employer is looking for is evidence that you will be a successful member of their team. The people they choose or invent for these profiles are a range of what they consider to be ideal employees. If you can show you have similar skills, abilities, interests and attitudes, then your application is more likely to be successful.

Where employers provide this sort of information and support, you will put yourself at a disadvantage if you have not made use of it. They will expect the results of having completed thorough self-analysis and company research to be reflected in your application and be evident in the way you perform at interview. It will help you decide if the work is suitable for you, and you for it. If your certainty of that can be communicated effectively, your application will be convincing.

Figure 2.3 Shell's site contains detailed employee profiles. Names act as a link to more detailed personal information.

SITES WORTH SEEING

Key words for searching the Web

- Psychometric tests.
- Personality tests.
- Aptitude tests.
- IQ tests.
- Verbal/numerical/mechanical/spatial reasoning tests.
- Self-assessment.
- Vocational interest inventories.

These key words can be used on search engines to help locate tests. Try including the word 'free' and your country name in searches. If you know the name of the test you wish to take/prepare for, enter that.

When looking at sites that offer free or priced tests, take particular note of their origin. Doing a test online can mean revealing some very personal details. You need to know what the organization or individual at the other end represents and what they will do with the information. If you can't find the details you need on the site, e-mail them. Most sites have a contact section or give an e-mail address.

Sites providing help with preparation for selection tests

As testing is a common feature in graduate recruitment, the sites that deal with this subject offer good practical tips on how to prepare for selection tests. Those listed below are freely available to all users, regardless of academic achievement. These come from a range of geographical locations and have been chosen because the information they contain is of value to all users.

If you have a problem accessing specific pages, use the first part of the URL (see under Locating sites and pages, Appendix A) to access that site's home page and search its contents section.

Gradlink

http://www.gradlink.edu.au

This is an Australian graduate careers guidance site. It gives excellent information and tips on all types of selection tests.

Graduate Horizons

http://www.ivision.co.uk/arcadia/horizons/
careers/psychom_tests.html

Detailed help pages on psychometric testing.

University of London Careers Service

http://www.careers.lon.ac.uk/helpshts/psycho.htm

Find help sheets on how to cope with aptitude tests and personality questionnaires.

Sites offering free access to self-assessment tools

The majority of sites listed below offer self-assessment exercises that prompt you to think about and build an accurate profile of yourself. These are not tests, but tools to guide you through the process. They should be printed off and worked through at your leisure. Tests that are completed online can be submitted to the host for scoring. The result usually comes back straight away. In some cases you need an e-mail address to receive this.

Birkman Quiz

http://cgi.review.com/birkman/ivillage/index.cfm

The 'Career Style Summary' provides a short personality-type questionnaire based on the Birkman Method – a tool for assessing interests, motivations, styles and stress behaviours.

The Braintainment Center

http://www.brain.com

Offers 'tests, info and tools to better understand and use your head to get ahead'. Free five-minute online IQ test. Other materials are priced.

Careersoft

http://www.careersoft.co.uk/seek/info/self_as.htm

UK careers software publisher. Its materials are widely available in schools and careers centres. The URL above gives access to a short but effective self-assessment exercise. The site has other extracts of its priced products, which are particularly useful for school-leavers and younger jobseekers.

The College Board

http://www.collegeboard.org/career/html/
searchQues.html

US association of schools and colleges, the aim of which is to facilitate student transition to higher education. This URL takes you to a career questionnaire that, when completed online, generates a list of careers that match your interests and abilities. Matches relate to the US job market.

GTI

http://www.gti.co.uk

UK publisher of graduate career guides. Short but effective self-assessment exercises can be found in the 'Just The Job' section.

INTEC

http://www.intec.edu.za/career/career.htm

South African college offering free online access and scoring of an interest inventory/personality test called CareerMatch. Six of your most significant personality attributes are matched against similar profiles for 100 different careers. From this it establishes which of those careers are well-suited to your personality.

Keirsey Temperament Sorter

http://keirsey.com

Almost every site on the Web that deals with personality testing has links to this one. Professor Keirsey, who developed the test, is an American clinical psychologist. The test is completed and scored online. It can be completed in English, Spanish or

German. An excellent site with extensive explanatory material and links to information on issues surrounding personality testing. To fully understand the test and your results, you should read the supporting book, *Please Understand Me*. Extracts and details of how to obtain it are on the site.

Minnesota Department of Economic Security
http://webserver.dsmd.state.al.us
This is part of America's Job Bank, but can be accessed directly using the URL above. The 'Creative Job Search' section has an excellent range of self-assessment exercises in worksheet form. These are applicable to all jobseekers, regardless of level or geographical location. They are useful for new entrants to the labour market, those wanting to change their job and those affected by redundancy. There are links to a related news group.

Schoolfinder
http://www.schoolfinder.com/careers/interest/index.htm and/or
http://www.schoolfinder.com/careers/aptitude/index.htm
Provides aptitude and interest quizzes that can be completed and scored online.

Two H
http://www.2h.com
A Swedish site with extensive links, some to light-hearted quizzes, others to respected tests. In their words, 'The tests listed here are just for your amusement . . . or frustration. Results should not be taken too literally. To get a valid result you should take a real test.'

University Of Pennsylvania
http://www.cdp.wharton.upenn.edu/accompli.htm and/or
http://www.cdp.wharton.upenn.edu/reschang.htm
These URLs take you to pages in the guidance section that have

excellent skills assessment exercises, including one on transferable skills aimed at career changers. They are relevant to all users, regardless of academic achievement, age or location.

University of Waterloo, Canada

http://www.adm.uwaterloo.ca:80/infocecs/CRC/
manual/introduction.html
The excellent 'Career Development Manual' can be accessed at this site. The self-assessment section contains detailed exercises you can print off. These guide you through assessing your knowledge, skills, interests, values, personality traits and achievements. The whole manual is worth looking at.

Youthworks

http://www.youthworks.ca/yw-pride.htm
This is a Canadian site that takes you through exercises to help you find the type of work that 'uses your talents and reflects your values and interests'. These are unusual and interesting. They are of particular relevance to younger jobseekers who are without higher-level qualifications.

Priced testing services

The best way to find these is through a local Web directory. Those listed below are not from commercial organizations.

Prospects Web

http://www.prospects.csu.ac.uk
This is a long-established and well-respected UK graduate careers information provider and publisher. A postal version of its interest inventory, Gradscope, can be ordered by e-mail from this site. At £12, it's much cheaper than similar services offered by commercial organizations.

Mensa

http://www.mensa.org.uk/mensa/psytests.html
This is the international society for people with high IQs, but it offers personality tests and interest inventories to anyone! These are priced, with a reduction in cost for members. Charges are much lower than those for similar services offered by commercial organizations. This site also gives access to free online IQ tests. These are primarily an advertising and recruiting tool for Mensa.

Sources of academic, research and background information on psychometric tests

Macquarie University Psychology Department

http://www.bhs.mq.edu.au/lib/testref.html
An Australian university with an extensive psychological tests library. Brief descriptions of tests are available on the web site. University of Chicago has something similar at http://stax.lib.uchicago.edu/LibInfo/Libraries/Tests

University of California

http://sunsite.unc.edu/personality
This site gives access to material on issues surrounding personality testing.

American Psychological Association

http://www.apa.org/science/test.html
These pages deal with questions that are frequently asked about psychological tests.

Employers offering help with self-assessment

Many employers include exercises or information that can help with the process. Some good examples include the following.

Hewlett-Packard

http://www-europe.hp.com
Look at the section on 'The HP Way'.

Asda, Sainsbury and Marks & Spencer

http://www.asda.co.uk
http://www.j-sainsbury.co.uk
http://www.marks-and-spencer.co.uk/recruit
These companies include employee profiles on their web sites.

KPMG

http://www.kpmg.co.uk
KPMG includes an exercise in self-assessment specific to its needs.

Shell International

http://www.shell.com
Shell invites you to treat the whole of its site as a self-assessment exercise and guides you through exercises that can then be used to help you complete its application form. It has interesting employee profiles.

SUMMARY

- Self-assessment is the starting point in the career decision-making and planning process.
- Effective self-assessment enables you to be focused and realistic in your choices. It is an essential part of the preparation you need to undertake to be able to communicate your potential to others.
- The WWW gives access to sites that can help with self-assessment and preparation for formal assessment by employers. An understanding of the purpose and appropriate use of tests is needed to evaluate their relevance for you and your situation.
- By preparing for formal tests, you can work more quickly and confidently.

Researching Careers

This chapter shows you how to research the jobs or career areas that match your skills, abilities and aspirations. It contains guidelines to help you evaluate the quality of information you will find on the web, and select that which will enable you to be focused, well informed and realistic in planning how to get from where you are now to where you want to be.

- Sources of careers information
- Careers information on the Web
- Evaluating information
- Action planning
- Sites worth seeing
- Summary

SOURCES OF CAREERS INFORMATION

Careers information can and should come from a range of sources, to help you construct a complete picture of what a job involves. In order to be of value, it must meet certain standards. It is of no use to find out how teachers were trained 20 years ago – things have changed. Information needs to be up to date, it should also be accurate, impartial, and comprehensive. If it's not, it can do more harm than good. It's up to you to check and evaluate the standard of any material you use. The easiest way is to look at who's providing it, their reasons for doing so and the date they did it.

Possible sources of information include the following:

- **Careers libraries in schools, colleges, universities.** An obvious place to start. They have a range of printed, video and computer-based material, selected because it meets quality standards. Information is classified by job and occupational area, so you'll find all the information on one career area together and it will signpost you to related information.
- **Professional associations and journals.** Many professional associations offer careers information and advice and publish journals. Reading professional journals can give you a good insight into ongoing concerns and new developments.
- **People doing the job you are interested in.** Talking to a number of different people doing the job you're interested in could help. However, you will only be gathering information on their personal experiences and everyone's experience is different. This is about as far from impartial information as you can get, but it is a good source of knowledge regarding finding openings and the negative aspects of a job or career area. For some career areas, however, it can be difficult to find enough people to talk to.
- **Job advertisements, job descriptions and person specifications.** These enable you to see what real employers are looking for right now. They give you details of the day-to-day work in an actual job, the qualifications and experience needed and the current rates of pay. The closing date shows you how up to date the information is. You can look at an advertisement and ask for a job description even if you've no intention of applying for that job. Trying to find vacancies to look at in the area that interests you will help show you whether jobs are abundant or a rarity.
- **TV programmes, films and novels that portray people at work.** People who write these usually painstakingly research the occupational area of their characters. You can benefit from their work. Again, it's not impartial, but it can give

you a good feel for what it's really like and show the downside of jobs that can often be overglamorized.

● **Work experience, work shadowing, visits to employers.** Employers are often happy to allow those seriously considering a career in their area of work to do some or all of the above. There's nothing better than trying it out for yourself to see if it suits you. This way you'll see both the positive and negative aspects. Entry to training for teaching and physiotherapy, for example, has related work experience as a prerequisite.

● **Employers and employment agencies.** Employers and employment agencies that specialize in particular occupations often produce information on it. They have an interest in getting people to do this type of work so their information is not entirely impartial. However, they do need to get the right person for the job, so they have to be accurate. Information is generally comprehensive and up to date.

● **Promotional organizations.** Many occupational areas have organizations the aim of which is to promote that career area to new entrants, such as the Teacher Training Agency and the Construction Industry Training Board. Their material may not be impartial, but it's accurate and comprehensive and aims to get the right sort of people interested in the work. It rarely mentions any of the negative aspects of the work.

● **The WWW.** This can give you easy access to all the above.

CAREERS INFORMATION ON THE WEB

The advantage of using Web-based careers information is that you will have access to information that is more up to date and comprehensive than that held in any careers library. You can probably find details of just about every job that exists in the industrialized nations, but will need to look at the source and decide how well it meets the standards described later in this chapter.

Web-based sources of information are just an adaptation of those described above.

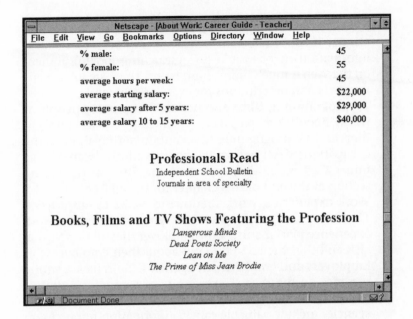

Figure 3.1 AboutWork takes a novel approach to careers information.

- **Careers libraries in schools, colleges, universities.** Increasingly, these can be accessed on the Web. Most universities, colleges and careers centres make at least part of their careers pages available to any user. These offer excellent general and job-specific careers advice.
- **Professional associations and journals.** Many professional and trade associations have web sites. An ever-increasing number of journals and newspapers are available in electronic form. There are sites that list them and provide links to them or you can use a search engine to find the more obscure ones. Many also make vacancy details available on the Web.
- **People doing the job you are interested in.** You can 'talk' to people using the Internet via programs such as Internet Relay Chat or communicate in writing by means of newsgroups. Employer sites and general guidance sites often have detailed personal profiles of people doing a range of jobs.

- **Job advertisements, job descriptions and person specifications.** If you're reluctant to write to employers for detailed information on jobs you're just researching, looking at them on the Web is much more anonymous. There are job advertisements and descriptions for every area of work.
- **TV programmes, films and novels that portray people at work.** AboutWork (see Figure 3.1) includes details of novels, films and TV programmes that contain portrayals of all the occupations described in its extensive jobs database (see under Careers guidance sites in the Sites worth seeing section at the end of this chapter for the address).
- **Work experience, work shadowing, visits to employers.** There are many sites that give you contacts for work experience placements. Some employer sites allow a virtual visit and the chance to find out about their employees.
- **Employers and employment agencies.** Both have a strong presence on the Web. The majority of corporate Web sites have careers information sections. The large employment agencies include valuable careers information resources on their sites.
- **Promotional organizations.** These organizations exist for many career areas and most have sites on the Web.

The links that sites develop means that preconceptions about what any organization has to offer can be wrong. Employment agencies do not just list jobs on the Web, they also give careers advice and labour market information; most employers do a lot more than just tell you about their products or vacancies.

EVALUATING INFORMATION

If you are accessing the information yourself, rather than through a careers adviser (or if you are the careers adviser), then you need to check its standard.

Is it comprehensive?

Comprehensive information will give you answers to the following questions.

- What skills and qualities are required?
- What are the entry requirements? These should include details of:
  — age (upper and lower limits)
  — qualifications
  — experience
  — health requirements and restrictions
  — geographical implications (need for mobility or proximity to an airport or fire station, for example, can be a prerequisite)
  — other significant factors (such as need for security clearance)
  — nationality or residency requirements.
- How competitive is entry to training/the job? Are opportunities on the increase or decrease?
- Who are the main employers?
- What are the promotion/development prospects?
- What's the work like on a day-to-day basis? What does a typical day/week consist of? Is the work repetitive or varied?
- What are the lifestyle implications of doing such work? Will time be spent away from home? Does it involve being in dangerous situations? Does it expose you to health hazards?
- Is there an international element to the work?
- Are opportunities for this type of work concentrated in particular regions or countries or are they widely available?
- Where can further information be obtained?
- Where are vacancies advertised?
- Are there opportunities for work experience, work shadowing or voluntary work?
- What are the related jobs and career areas?

Is it impartial?

Impartiality is harder to quantify. You have to ask yourself what is the purpose of the organization or individual presenting the information. An organization promoting careers in the health services is not impartial, whereas a site offering general information on graduate careers is (unless it's being sponsored by a health service provider!) Of course you need to look at information that is promoting a positive image of a profession that interests you, but be aware that it is not impartial.

Is it accurate?

Accuracy can be difficult to judge, too. You don't know if what appears to be accurate really is until you start using it. Things to look out for include the following.

● Accuracy of addresses, phone numbers and other links mentioned.
● If there is detailed information on entry requirements, check that the qualifications mentioned include the most recent additions and changes to your country's assessment system.
● If pay rates are included, is there a date given for when they applied?
● If there is information on labour market factors, such as job prospects and skill shortages, is there a date when this information was gathered and is the source given?
● If the job described is overglamorized, it may be less than accurate. Descriptions that show progression from tea lady to chief executive don't always ring true and should be treated with caution.

Any accurate description of a job or career area should mention some of the bad as well as the good aspects of doing such work. It is unlikely that any one source of information will contain material that meets all these criteria – you have to gather and evaluate information from a variety of sources to get a complete picture.

ACTION PLANNING

There is so much information available on the Web that researching and using it needs to be approached in a logical and systematic manner. One way of doing this is to make an action plan. If you make a shopping list, you are composing a sort of action plan in that it forms a structured reminder of what you need to do. Researching entry to one or more career areas means dealing with a range of information from a variety of sources. This inevitably highlights further things you need to do and research. Making an action plan keeps you focused and helps you set realistic, achievable targets. It is particularly important when researching on the Web as it will prevent you getting side-tracked and distracted.

It doesn't matter what format your plan takes. Initially, you should make one detailing what you need to research. When your research has been completed, you will be in a position to formulate a career plan that will outline the steps you need to take to achieve your goals. If you have access to a careers adviser, they will help you formulate such plans. Alternatively, you can work through the following steps to produce one yourself.

Research plan

- Write one or two sentences that describe your current position.
- Having completed self-assessment exercises, write down your ultimate goals.
- List three jobs that you think would suit you well, and as many employers as you can think of that you would like to work for.
- Find and list web sites that offer careers information related to your interests, and relevant employer sites.
- List all the things you need to know more about. Select items listed under the heading Evaluating information earlier in this chapter to compose your own list.

Using this, bookmark sites you wish to visit for your research (see under Navigation Aids, Appendix A). Print off the information you gather and use it to answer the questions you have previously identified. Avoid the temptation to look at just one more link – it can lead to never-ending research. Delete from your list and bookmarks web sites that were not as useful as they sounded. Once you have answers to the questions on your list, move on to producing a career plan.

Career plan

- Start by making a clear statement of your long-term goals.
- Carry out an analysis of why they represent realistic choices. This should include details of how your interests, skills, qualifications, personal characteristics and experience match the requirements of the job(s) you are targeting.
- Identify gaps in your qualifications or experience.
- Construct a timetable for filling these gaps and details of resources that will help you do this.
- Make a list of the most valuable sources of information you found on the Web that you wish to revisit.
- List sites that advertise vacancies or training opportunities in your chosen area.
- If you have applied for jobs or registered your CV with any sites, include details of passwords that were issued to enable you to access your information another time.
- Make a list of all the things you have to do to move closer to your goal. Include a timescale for each action point.
- Review and revise your plan regularly.

SITES WORTH SEEING

The sites described below represent a small sample of some of the best resources on the Web. They have been selected to offer a taste of what is available. As each links to other sites, there are potentially thousands of places to visit using only the URLs listed here. Initially, therefore, make an action plan listing two or three sites that are of most relevance to you, and keep your search focused on them alone.

Careers guidance sites

Many of the best sites are linked to educational institutions, state employment offices and careers centres. Such providers usually ensure that the information is comprehensive, impartial and accurate. Although sites in the country where you are seeking work are of the greatest relevance, it can be worth looking at others for their special features.

All universities have web sites, and most have sections devoted to the activities of their careers services. Some of the vacancy information is only available to students, but other information related to career planning and job hunting is freely available and of excellent quality. Sites providing links to all UK universities include Prospects Web, Datalake (see under Publishers of careers material below for the address) and Career Mosaic (see under Employment agencies in the Sites worth seeing section of Chapter 4 for the address).

AboutWork: Career Database

http://www.aboutwork.com/career/index.html

An American site with a wide range of information that is of value to jobseekers worldwide. There is an interesting section giving 'a day in the life of' information on a whole range of careers. Although salary details and other statistics are from the US, additional information – such as books, TV shows and films that portray people doing the job you are interested in – has international interest. The site also offers self-assessment exercises, access to chat groups on employment-related matters and help with application techniques.

America's Job Bank

http://www.ajb.dni.us

One of the most extensive databases of current vacancies in the US, this site also gives access to a range of quality careers information that is of relevance to all, regardless of location.

CanDo: Disability Careers Network

http://cando.lancs.ac.uk

CanDo is the national British careers web site for disabled university students and graduates. The site includes general careers information, employer profiles, current vacancies, details of special employment schemes and work experience opportunities.

Careers Guidance Resources on the Web

http://www.unn.ac.uk/~ecu1

This is a site aimed at advisers, teachers, librarians and others researching careers information. It does not contain careers information, but has links to a huge number of sites that do, with brief descriptions of what they offer. It is particularly useful for its international links and sites related to specific careers areas. These are classified using the Careers Library Classification Index (CLCI), the system used by schools and careers centres in the UK. It is only updated a few times a year, so links are sometimes out of date.

Career Resource Center

http://www.careers.org

This is an extensive index of US and Canadian careers-related web sites. It has over 7500 links to related sites, including employers, vacancy sections of newspapers, employment-related news groups, state employment offices, careers centres and employment agencies.

Prospects Web

http://www.prospects.csu.ac.uk

CSU is an agency responsible for collecting and disseminating information on graduate recruitment in the UK. It provides a link between employers, university careers services and graduate jobseekers. There are over 400 detailed job descriptions, clearly marked with the date they were written and when they will next be updated. The emphasis is on graduate-level jobs, but these cover some for which a degree is not essential, such as air cabin crew, police and ambulance work. In addition to general information, there is a searchable database of around 1500 graduate employers. Current vacancies are advertised on the site. There are links to all UK higher education careers services that have web sites, overseas sites offering guidance, vacancy information for new graduates and gateway sites in other countries.

Search

http://www.careersite-search.org.uk

A good example of one of the many careers centre sites in the UK. These centres primarily provide advice and guidance for school and college leavers, but some also offer services to adults. Indeed, this site contains a wide range of job fact sheets that are of value to all. Links to other UK careers companies with web sites can be found at the Datalake site (see under Publishers of careers information below for the address) or the DFEE's Choice and Careers Division site at:

http://www.open.gov.uk/dfee/ccd/csaddres.htm

Appointments to see an adviser can often be made via careers centre web sites.

The site

http://www.thesite.org.uk

A comprehensive gateway to links that are likely to be of interest to young people. It covers topics such as health, housing, and leisure time activities as well as careers related issues. It has extensive links to local organizations providing help with a range of concerns. It won an award for the best non-commercial website of 1997.

SYO-Guiden

http://www.pedc.se/syo/utnavbar.html
This is a Swedish site that can be viewed in different European languages, including English. It has an excellent index of links to careers guidance sites worldwide.

Professional bodies, training organizations and examining bodies

A growing number of these organizations have web sites that provide comprehensive and accurate careers information. Examples include the following.

British National Space Centre – Space Index

http://www.highview.co.uk
The Space Index is a directory of space-related activities in the UK and further afield. It contains careers information, details of related events and links to listings of space-related jobs.

British Psychological Society

http://www.bps.org.uk/careers/careers.htm
Here, you can find detailed information on careers and training in psychology.

British Medical Journal

http://www.bmj.com
The Career Focus section contains archives of careers-related articles. This is an excellent site for researching the implications of a career in medicine at the decision-making stage, as well as being a source of information to aid career development. Articles cover a wide range of topics, such as working in New Zealand, job sharing, the availability of flexible training for those with families, how to move into medical broadcasting, and what sort of work to look for if you need regular sleep.

English Nursing Board

http://www.enb.org.uk
The ENB careers service provides information, advice and guidance for anyone who is interested in a career in nursing or midwifery. This site also provides information for nurses and midwives who have qualified overseas and are interested in working in the UK.

Council in Europe

http://www.ciee.org/europe/index.htm
This site offers work experience, short-term jobs and exchange programmes in a wide range of countries for students and recent graduates. Each year, over 20,000 students – the majority of them Europeans – participate in these programmes. Schemes include the Japan Exchange and Teaching programme (JET) and the US Internship scheme, which allows some 4000 students annually to work in the USA for 6 months.

National Council for the Training of Journalists

www.itecharlow.co.uk
Here you can find detailed information on careers and training in journalism and photojournalism.

The Chartered Institute of Banking

http://www.cib.org.uk/careers.html
The institute provides material to help with career planning and job hunting in banking and finance in the UK.

Nahat Gateway to the Internet

http://www.nahat.net/gateway.htm
This is an index to all medically related matters, which is useful for those researching specific careers in this area. It has a UK bias, but links worldwide.

Publishers of careers material

Careersoft
http://www.careersoft.co.uk
This is a good site for younger jobseekers. It contains extracts from its priced material, which is widely available in careers centres, schools and colleges.

Datalake
http://westlake.co.uk/datalake
This site has a wide range of UK careers information and employment opportunities for new entrants to the labour market from school, college and university. A wide range of career areas is covered and some vacancy and sponsorship details are given. The site gives contact details for all UK professional and industry lead bodies, and all UK careers service providers. It hosts a site for the National Association of Careers and Guidance Teachers. It started out as a navigator to university resources worldwide, and aims to eventually make possible subject searches of all higher education courses throughout the world. There is extensive course information and it is possible to order prospectuses and apply online for postgraduate courses.

Gradunet
http://www.gradunet.co.uk
This UK site has a wealth of information and links, including details of industrial and summer placements. It contains career profiles of students who've been successful in finding work, and has a discussion group on careers-related issues. It also has a useful up-to-date calendar of recruitment fairs and events.

GTI Careerscape
http://www.gti.co.uk
Astronaut or accountant? Philosopher or pet food taster? GTI claims to let you know what jobs are really like. Updated every week, it has lively information on all careers-related matters and lots of useful links.

Employers

The sites of many employers, both large and small, offer a wealth of careers information. What this may lack in impartiality is made up for by its accuracy and up-to-date content. The sites listed below have been chosen to reflect the variety of what is available. The best way to find an employer's web site is by referring to one of the large business directories on the Web that provides links to company sites and allows you to search by name or sector.

For the UK try the following.

The Biz

http://www.thebiz.co.uk or UK Business Net
http://www.ukbusinessnet.com
Both sites provide basic company information, hypertext links to companies that have web sites and contact information for those that don't.

For US and global companies, look at the following.

Hoover's corporate web sites

http://www.hoovers.com
Hoover has links to web sites for more than 5000 of the world's largest companies. It is possible to search just for those that have job listings. Looking at job descriptions for current vacancies is an excellent way of getting up-to-date information, even if you're years away from applying for such a post. It will help you identify what you need for such work and help you make informed decisions about choice of courses and work experience.

BBC World of Careers

http://www.bbc.co.uk
An excellent resource for researching all matters related to broadcasting. The BBC World of Careers section contains a set of factsheets providing comprehensive information on every

career available with the company. Each page links to current vacancies in that career area, information on related training available, relevant publications and other sites that may be of interest.

The World of Training gives information on current training opportunities, details of major training schemes and media-related courses run by the BBC that are open to the public. Included in this section is information on graduate sponsorship schemes, the broadcast journalist and news trainee schemes and opportunities for vacation training and placements.

KPMG

http://www.kpmg.co.uk/uk/career

The careers section on this site gives a thorough overview of what it takes to be an accountant, answering questions such as 'Aren't accountancy and consultancy boring jobs filled with boring people?' 'Banging, stomping, thumping, hardcore techno-jungle. Is there anyone at KPMG who knows what that means?' (One has the answer 'Yes' and the other, 'No'. Visit the site to see if you got it right!)

Marks & Spencer

http://www.marks-and-spencer.co.uk

Most major retailers have web sites. This one offers detailed careers and self-assessment information for potential applicants. Careers in business management, food technology and IT are on offer. It also has a Business Placement Programme, which is salaried and open to all those on sandwich courses, lots of company information, a summary of the principles that guide the company, financial summaries, overviews of the year's performance and an interactive branch locator designed to help you find details of any Marks & Spencer store in the world. There is also information on the careers fairs it attends and details of in-store careers presentations.

Shell International

http://www.shell.com

An excellent site that is worth a visit even if you have no interest in working for Shell. There is lots of company and careers information, employee profiles and links to all their other sites worldwide. There's the Common Room where you can discuss careers-related queries, a News Room that gives access to global online newspapers, EUNI, which lists all UK universities and has information on student matters, Bookzone, which is a place where you can find 'unusual and intelligent' books, and Centre for the Slightly Amused, 'a whacky, amusing site of silliness'. The links a company includes in its sites tells you a lot about them. They can make a good talking point at interview!

Employment agencies

Many agencies offer information on labour market trends and a range of careers information. Employment agency sites are also listed at the end of Chapter 4.

The Monster Board

http://www.monster.com and/or
http://www.monster.co.uk

The advice for visitors to this site is that 'Life's short. And, unfortunately, work's a big part of it. Better enjoy what you do.' In addition to advertising vacancies, the site provides a range of services to help you achieve this. There are the Monster Board's communities – 'cyber societies' created for people interested in specific career areas. Each community provides information on the latest industry trends and opportunities to network with colleagues online, along with interactive surveys and topics for discussion. If you're looking at jobs using the UK site, link to the US one for a look at their careers information resource – it has many items that are of international interest. Monster has sites in Canada, Australia, Belgium and The Netherlands and more are planned for the future. Once you're in one, you can access all the others.

TV Jobs

http://www.tvjobs.com/intern.htm
Here you will find lists of a large number of US TV companies offering work experience placements. Global links are being developed.

Others

Teacher Training Agency

http://www.teach.org.uk
The Agency's aim is to attract more people into teaching. The information given is accurate, comprehensive and up to date, but not impartial. The site includes help for mature students, a course search facility, profiles of people in the profession, details of grants and salaries and links to all institutions offering initial teacher training in England and Wales.

The Washington Post

http://www.washingtonpost.com/wp-adv/
classifieds/careerpost/parachute/front.htm
This site has interesting articles on using the WWW for career development purposes, reviews of major US guidance sites and links to them.

Youthnet

http://www.youthnet.org.uk
This site provides help or advice on a wide range of topics, including careers for young people in the UK. Its stated aim is to 'help you quickly find the right organization in the right place, whatever you are looking for.' It has lots of useful links.

SUMMARY

- To gain a comprehensive picture of a career area, your information on it should come from a variety of sources.
- For information to be of value, it needs to be accurate and up to date.
- It is important to be able to distinguish between information that is impartial and that which is not. Both kinds are needed to help create a comprehensive picture.
- The WWW gives access to information on most careers. The quality of information varies and needs to be evaluated by the user.
- Researching to find information and then using it to formulate career goals requires a logical and systematic approach.

How and Where to Find Vacancies on the Web

This chapter will enable you to harness the potential of having access to millions of job openings in a focused and manageable way. Vacancies are not just for jobseekers, they are an excellent resource for investigating careers.

- Looking for vacancies
- Sources of advertised vacancies on the Web
- Sites worth seeing
- Summary

LOOKING FOR VACANCIES

Finding suitable jobs to apply for is a time-consuming business. Many people stay in a job they dislike because they don't have the time to look for another. Searching through vacancies on the Web could leave you with no time to apply for work. On the other hand, if you know where to look and what to do, it can result in vacancies and employers finding you!

The main sources of advertised vacancies on the Web are the same as they always have been. This medium simply offers greater access to a wider range of information. Advertisements for current vacancies are found in newspapers, professional journals and institutes, recruitment agencies and from employers themselves. Each of these sources can be used in different ways or in combination depending on your circumstances. If you want a job in a specific location, look at the recruitment pages in your local paper. For a job in a particular professional field or trade, look in the professional or trade journal for that occupation. If you are really keen to work for a specific employer, find out all you can about them.

Vacancies advertised on the Web are clearly for people who can use this medium. The jobs were initially IT-related, but now it's true to say that every industry's vacancies can be found there. Every occupational sector has been affected by IT, and computer literacy is becoming the job requirement that ordinary literacy was a generation ago.

Passive job hunting – helping jobs find you

Normally, trying to find the right vacancies requires you to constantly monitor a range of suitable sources. Only a privileged few can sit back and feel assured that employers will come looking for them because their talents and capabilities are known. However, the Web makes it possible for everyone to become a passive jobseeker! Sadly this does not mean that you can do nothing at all and find an offer of the perfect job among your e-mails, but it is getting close.

Employment agencies have always made passive job hunting possible. They store your CV and contact you with suitable vacancies. Now, most large agencies and many small ones do a substantial proportion of their recruiting by means of the Web. Some, such as The Monster Board (see Figures 4.1 and 4.2), only exist on the Web. Newspapers and even employers with web sites are offering 'passive' job hunting facilities. The slogan for *The Guardian*'s RecruitNet site is 'Let the job find you', and its Early Bird option e-mails you with suitable vacancy advertisements. Some employers invite detailed speculative applications that are then stored for considerable periods and matched against vacancies as they occur. 'We'll keep you on file' really means something with a growing number of employers.

There are various degrees of passivity. Registering with newspaper sites, such as *The Guardian*, or Job Hunter takes very little

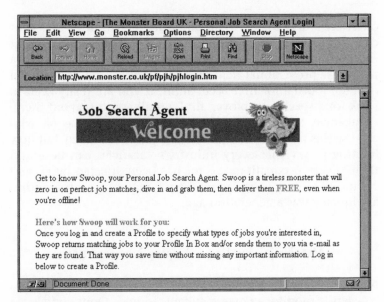

Figure 4.1 The Monster Board's job search takes the hard work out of the hunt for a job.

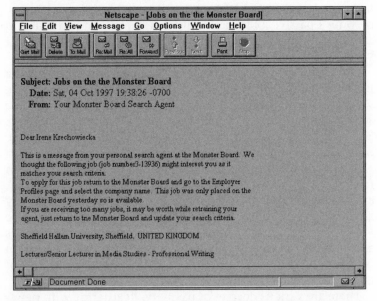

Figure 4.2 The agent keeps you informed of progress by e-mail.

thought or effort. You simply select your job criteria via a series of drop-down menus. In return, vacancies that match your specified choices will be e-mailed to you. This will not get you a job directly, but will prevent you from missing an advertisement that you might like to investigate further. With employers such as Microsoft, you need to put considerable effort into making an initial application, but there's then no need to contact them again for a year in order to be considered for jobs. Employment agencies come somewhere in between these two ends of the spectrum. Their initial registration forms are not usually as detailed as those of employers, but are detailed enough to enable more specific matching than the newspaper sites.

A job search done in this way can yield good results that seem disproportionate to the effort invested. It is particularly useful for those who have little time left to scan advertisements, those who are geographically mobile, those who want a job in another area or country and those who are vaguely thinking about changing jobs or looking for work and want to see what's out there without spending too long investigating the situation.

CV banks and databases

You can use the Web as a place to display your CV to thousands of potential employers. Most employment agencies offer the facility for you to register a CV with them for a specified amount of time. It is then made available to employers. Your CV is normally treated as confidential information, and would not initially show personal details without your authorization of such disclosure. It is possible to deny access to certain employers (useful if you don't want your current employer to see that you are looking for a new job) or opt for complete availability. You could display your CV on your own web site or use one of the many sites where the sole purpose is the display of jobseekers' CVs. Which option you choose depends on how you feel about having your personal details made known to the world. Information Providers Limited's (IPL) site (see under Gateway sites in the Sites worth seeing section at the end of this chapter for the address) includes a listing of recruitment companies in the UK that accept CVs for their databases. See Chapter 5 for details on how to prepare your CV for inclusion on agency sites and public databases.

Active job hunting

If you're after a job sooner rather than later, you need to actively look for additional vacancies. The easiest to find are those that are advertised. Examples of sites that give access to these are listed and described at the end of this chapter. Those that have large numbers of vacancies usually have sophisticated search facilities to help you quickly identify the jobs that are relevant to you.

In addition to giving access to advertised vacancies, the Web can facilitate non-intrusive contact with employers. If you are really keen to work for a particular company, but there are no vacancies when you first contact them, you may be reluctant to try again every day for six months. That could be one way of making certain they never offered you an interview! However, only contacting them at six-weekly intervals could mean you miss the opportunity to apply for your dream job. If you look at their web site every day, you won't be causing a nuisance and yet you will be certain to see that vacancy you need to know about when it occurs. The BBC, for example, encourages this approach by suggesting that you bookmark the page where jobs that interest you will appear and visit it regularly.

Speculative applications

Some employers, such as Hewlett-Packard, Microsoft and Shell, positively encourage speculative applications via their web sites. Others actively discourage it. Try anything like that with BT, for example, and you get a very curt e-mail in return. There are also many employers who don't mention recruitment on their web sites, but provide information that you can use to help convince them they need you. As the number of companies with web sites increases, so does the opportunity to be more creative in your search for a job.

It is estimated that the majority of all vacancies are not publicly advertised. Well-researched speculative applications can therefore yield good results. The way company information is organized on the Web can make it easy to identify and thoroughly research potential employers and individuals within companies who are worth targeting. This does not mean sending your basic CV to an employer on the off chance that there is something suitable. The research for such an application needs to be more detailed than that undertaken for a job that exists. You are aiming to show an employer that there is a need you can meet, when they didn't even know they had it! For help with constructing an effective CV, see Chapter 5.

SOURCES OF ADVERTISED VACANCIES ON THE WEB

If you are not sure of the best sources of information for your particular area of interest, start with one of the 'gateway' sites. These are sites that act as signposts by listing, describing and providing links to sites with vacancy information (see under Gateway Sites in the Sites Worth Seeing section at the end of this chapter).

Newspapers and journals

Newspapers are traditionally the first place jobseekers look for vacancies. They are an excellent source of focused information. Local newspapers cover defined geographical areas, national papers often specialize by concentrating on specific occupational sectors on different days of the week. The WWW has made newspapers all over the world easily and, in most cases, freely accessible. There are several sites that list and link to electronic newspapers and journals from around the world.

Several electronic newspapers have paid special attention to developing their vacancy sections. Many papers derive a substantial part of their revenue from advertising jobs, and regard Web-based recruiting as enhancing the service they offer to employers. If an employer is inundated with too many responses or does not receive enough, the advertisement will not have been effective in their terms. Comprehensive information to support an advertisement is often the key to eliciting effective responses. If it's clear what the requirements of the employer are, applicants are more likely to engage in accurate self-selection. It would be prohibitively expensive to include detailed job descriptions in newspaper advertisements, but when they are on web sites, they can include links to volumes of detail for little extra cost.

The use being made of such vacancy sites in the UK, where they are a relatively new phenomenon, is staggering. Every time a page is accessed it is logged as a 'hit' by the computer. Between the end of November 1996 and mid March 1997, *The Guardian's* RecruitNet site recorded nearly 5 million visits. That worked out as an average of 43,239 hits a day! Many of these will have been repeat visits, but this level of traffic is not unusual for sites advertising vacancies.

The online vacancy sections of newspapers usually allow you to browse for jobs on type of work, location, salary range or to conduct job-specific searches based on key word matching. Some offer additional facilities, including access to careers advice and e-mail notification of suitable vacancies (see Figure 4.3). This service is offered by many local as well as national newspapers.

Professional or trade journals are a good source of vacancy information in specialist fields. There is one for almost every occupation from architecture to zoology. The number of these that have web sites is growing rapidly. In addition to vacancies, sites give access to details of news, research and concerns affecting the occupational area they cover. Such sites are invaluable for pre-application research.

Employment agencies

The aim of employment agencies is to fill posts quickly with the best people available. They have two customers: the employer and the applicant. To meet the demands of both, they have to contain accurate, up-to-date information and offer help with the whole job-search and vacancy-filling process. As

Figure 4.3 Registration with *The Guardian*'s RecruitNet is free and you are offered a range of services to make job hunting easier.

a result, they offer potential applicants help with applying, researching, preparing for interviews and selection tests. Many have detailed careers information, current labour market information and links to discussion groups on job hunting-related topics. All this is of value even if you don't intend to apply for any of their jobs.

Employment agencies have been quick to see and utilize the potential of the Web. Such agencies offer employers access to a huge bank of potential applicants. Agencies get business from them because they can reach large numbers and conduct initial screening. Some agencies advertise vacancies applicants can search, some keep a bank of CVs for employers, others select and present short lists to employers. Most agencies offer free services to jobseekers. In some countries, such as the UK, it is illegal for an employment agency to charge for their services, with certain exceptions. If there is a fee, check if that organization has something significantly more valuable to offer you than one offering its services for free.

Employment agency sites have their own search engines that enable you to enter key words that are matched to current vacancies. You can search by location, salary, occupational area, contract, permanent, temporary work and so on. Most will e-mail you with details of jobs that match your criteria.

Most of the agencies on the Web are commercial organizations, but state employment agencies also make use of this technology. The largest, America's Job Bank, has excellent careers and labour market information. Similar sites are being created and maintained by European governmental agencies. Of the commercial companies, large concerns include The Monster Board, Career Mosaic, TAPS and Reed. Smaller agencies may specialize in particular occupational areas or skill levels. Some agencies have a physical presence; others only exist on the Web.

Employers

Employers need employees, vacancies originate from them and applicants end up being interviewed by them. The WWW allows employers to reach a huge audience without engaging intermediaries such as newspapers and agencies. It is a cheap and effective way to target computer-literate applicants who are demonstrating their motivation, initiative and confidence in the use of the new technologies by using them to search for vacancies. The 1997 Austin Knight *Internet Recruitment Survey* shows that increasing numbers of employers are moving to direct recruitment using their own web sites.

Most employers regard the increased number of applicants that their Web presence generates as a positive development. However, in the same way that unlimited vacancies can cause problems for jobseekers, unlimited applications can cause problems for employers. The ease of electronic communication should not tempt you to fire off multiple, ill-researched applications to all and sundry.

Many companies use their web sites to provide detailed information on themselves, their vacancies and what they require of employees. They do this to help applicants to self-select and be more realistic about the positions they apply for than would otherwise be possible. When an employer goes to the bother of maintaining a web site, there will also be an expectation that you have used it effectively, particularly if you are contacting them via that site. Employers have reported being frustrated at receiving e-mails containing questions on matters fully covered on their web sites. Asking questions that show you have not bothered to research your application properly or that you have problems understanding written information will not enhance your prospects of getting a job.

Employers that use their own web sites to encourage people to apply to them do so in a variety of ways. Some advertise specific vacancies and invite direct applications using a form that can be filled in on the screen and transmitted electronically. In many cases, such applications are read initially by screening software (see under Electronic applications, Chapter 5). Looking at a range of employers' sites can be useful, as the hints and tips each offers can help with your other applications (see Figure 5.4).

US companies have been using the WWW for recruitment for some time, and there is widespread use of electronic application systems. Use of online application systems by European companies is increasing. UK companies offering electronic application forms, such as the BBC and British Telecom, have a paper option, too.

Employers that use the Web as a recruitment tool without advertising specific vacancies give general company information and details such as recruitment procedures, entry requirements and employee profiles (see Figure 4.4). This gives valuable clues to the range of skills and other attributes they want to see highlighted in an application.

KPMG, for example, includes extensive recruitment information on its web site without advertising specific vacancies. The company has found that this results in fewer requests for application packs, but a higher proportion of those requesting packs are suitable for the posts they are targeting. Many companies that recruit new graduates take this approach on their web sites.

News groups

These are an additional source of vacancy information. Some deal with specific career areas, while others concentrate on

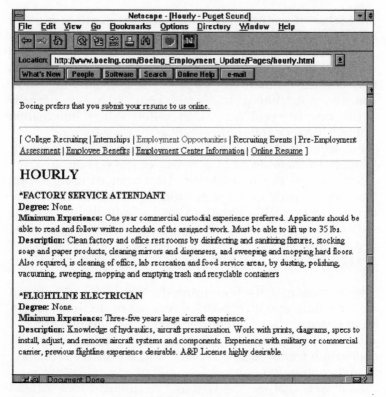

Netscape - [Hourly - Puget Sound]

File   Edit   View   Go   Bookmarks   Options   Directory   Window   Help

Location: http://www.boeing.com/Boeing_Employment_Update/Pages/hourly.html

What's New | People | Software | Search | Online Help | e-mail

Boeing prefers that you submit your resume to us online.

[College Recruiting | Internships | Employment Opportunities | Recruiting Events | Pre-Employment Assessment | Employee Benefits | Employment Center Information | Online Resume]

HOURLY

*FACTORY SERVICE ATTENDANT
Degree: None.
Minimum Experience: One year commercial custodial experience preferred. Applicants should be able to read and follow written schedule of the assigned work. Must be able to lift up to 35 lbs.
Description: Clean factory and office rest rooms by disinfecting and sanitizing fixtures, stocking soap and paper products, cleaning mirrors and dispensers, and sweeping and mopping hard floors. Also required, is cleaning of office, lab recreation and food service areas, by dusting, polishing, vacuuming, sweeping, mopping and emptying trash and recyclable containers

*FLIGHTLINE ELECTRICIAN
Degree: None.
Minimum Experience: Three-five years large aircraft experience.
Description: Knowledge of hydraulics, aircraft pressurization. Work with prints, diagrams, specs to install, adjust, and remove aircraft systems and components. Experience with military or commercial carrier, previous flightline experience desirable. A&P License highly desirable.

Document Done

Figure 4.4 Seattle-based Boeing advertises all its vacancies on the Web, from highly specialized technical posts to cleaning jobs, and says that it prefers to receive electronic resumés for all posts rather than paper ones.

geographical areas. Search for ones that are relevant to you using one of the search engines dedicated to news groups. Career Mosaic provides a link to jobs-related news groups via its site (see under Employment agencies in the Sites worth seeing section at the end of this chapter for the address).

The sheer number of vacancies on the Web could lead you to believe that all jobs are advertised there. That is not the case. Some jobs are advertised only on the Web, a growing number on the Web and elsewhere at the same time, but many only by a variety of methods, including word of mouth and networking. An effective vacancy search therefore calls for a combination of both old and new methods.

SITES WORTH SEEING

The sites listed below are a small selection that have been chosen to show a range of methods being used to attract and inform applicants.

Gateway sites

These are sites that provide links rather than offer vacancies. Accessing any one of these gives you hundreds of possibilities to explore.

Lifestyle UK

http://lifestyle.co.uk/bh.htm
A directory providing links to sites offering recruitment information. Links to vacancies in the media, accountancy, scientific, business, computing, hotels, restaurants, au pair work and much more. The majority are UK-based, but there are links to European and US sites, which then offer links to even more sites.

Information Providers Limited (IPL)

http://www.ipl.co.uk/recruit.html
This site provides an index of links to UK recruitment sites. There are also links to sites that act as CV banks.

Purdue University Placement Service (USA)

http://www.purdue.edu/ups/student/jobsites.htm
This American University site in Indiana has just over a thousand links to job searching sites, and claims to be the Internet's largest.

The Riley Guide to Employment Opportunities and Job Resources on the Internet
http://www.dbm.com/jobguide

A selection of the best US vacancy sites are also listed and comprehensively described by this guide, which gives you enough information to sort out job hunting in the US and many other places, too.

Newspapers and journals and related sources

Some newspapers and journals offer a subscription-only service and these are not included in the following list. All those below offer free access to vacancies.

World Newspapers
http://www.dds.nl/~kidon/papers.html

This Dutch site gives listings of, and links to, all the world's major newspapers. You can look at local vacancies from Alaska to Zimbabwe, and check the weather at the same time. This site is equally useful for looking at the Scottish, Irish or Lancashire papers.

E&P Directory of Online Newspapers
http://www.mediainfo.com/ephome/npaper/nphtm/online.htm

This claims to be the most comprehensive reference resource of its kind. It includes newspapers that are on the WWW as well as those available via proprietary online services. Web-based papers are listed by country, and for the US they are also listed by state. You can search for specific publications, locations or attributes.

Financial Times
http://www.FT.com

This site gives a range of finance and business related vacancies. It links to *The Daily Telegraph*, which can be accessed separately at http://www.telegraph.co.uk

The Guardian

http://recruitnet.guardian.co.uk

'Let the job find you'. Browse through all *The Guardian*'s jobs, get detailed job descriptions and, in some cases, link to employers' web sites or set up Early Bird, which will e-mail you daily with details of jobs matching your requirements. The search facility allows for selection by a range of criteria, including location and salary. Vacancies advertised here are generally of a professional nature, covering a wide range of occupational areas, including education, media, marketing, IT, environment and public service.

Irish Times

http://recruit.irish-times.com

This is a searchable site for jobs in Ireland.

Job Hunter

www.jobhunter.co.uk

Here you will find a compilation of vacancies from the UK's regional press. It claims to give access to tens of thousands of vacancies that are updated daily. Search profiles are matched against vacancies and details can be e-mailed to you on a daily basis for a fixed period. All regions of the UK are covered.

Overseas Jobs Express

http://www.overseasjobs.com

An electronic version of this fortnightly publication, with at least 1500 job vacancies being given in each publication. The site has over 700 links to employment resources in 40 countries. It has a link to a database of seasonal and summer jobs that can be accessed separately on http://www.summerjobs.com There is also a travel link, which provides a service for travellers wishing to find people to accompany them.

British Medical Journal
http://www.bmj.com
Free registration gives you access to a wide range of medical vacancies in the UK and elsewhere.

The Cell
http://server.cell.com/recruit
This is the international journal of the Biological Sciences. It has lots of vacancies that can be searched for by field, level and country or continent.

Construction Site
http://www.emap.com/construct
This site offers a wide selection of jobs selected from *The Architects' Journal*, *Construction News* and *New Civil Engineer*. This is updated weekly. Note that the main emap site offers links to a range of specialist journals (www.emap.com).

Dalton's Weekly
http://www.daltons.co.uk/busia.htm
This site specializes in the sale of businesses in the UK and overseas. It includes shops, residential care premises, pubs and clubs, catering businesses, hotels and guest houses, and franchises.

Fleet NewsNet
http://www2.automotive.co.uk
Current vacancies in fleet management, accident management, fuel management, contract hire, vehicle leasing, vehicle rental, automotive manufacturing and automotive imports can be found here.

Health Service Journal
http://www.hsj.co.uk
This is a weekly UK health policy and management magazine. Vacancies for medical, nursing, social work, research, personnel, health promotion and management jobs are listed at this site.

Local Government Chronicle

http://www.lgcnet.com
The comprehensive listing of local authority jobs here is up-dated weekly. Vacancies can be searched for by job type, employer type or salary level.

Marketing Online

http://www.marketing.haynet.com
This is a weekly listing of a wide range of marketing jobs. Marketing career files on over 300 companies that have placed advertisements with the magazine are available without charge for the first five requested.

Nature

http://www.nature.com
Here you will find comprehensive international science job listings, and these are updated weekly. Jobs are listed by subject, country, organization or position. There are links to employer profiles and details of conferences and fellowships.

New Scientist

http://www.newscientist.com
The Planet Science recruitment database is searchable and offers approximately 300 UK scientific, technological and academic vacancies a week. Searches can be made by employment category, discipline and key words. Lots of science-related news and articles and enhanced information on many of the articles in the printed version of the magazine can also be found here.

Physics World Jobs

http://www.iop.org./cgi-bin/Jobs/vacancies
Part of the UK's Institute of Physics' site, it is a regularly updated source of information on jobs and research opportunities. These are mainly in the UK, but some overseas opportunities are listed, too.

The Scientist
```
http://www.the-scientist.library.upenn.edu/
index.html
```
An American scientific journal, similar to *New Scientist*.

Employment agencies

America's Job Bank
```
http://www.ajb.dni.us
```
If you want to see what the future promises for state employment services, look at this site. It links all state employment service offices to provide one of the largest pools of current vacancies available anywhere. Each state's site has lots of quality careers information, details of labour market trends and links to other providers of vacancy information. There are extra facilities on some, such as CV databases. Jobs are for US residents only, but the additional information is of relevance to all.

Career Mosaic
```
http://www.careermosaic.com
```
A company described as 'reshaping the job-finding process'. It has separate sites for different parts of the world. The original, Career Mosaic USA, is now supplemented by Career Mosaic Asia, Australia, Canada, France, Hong Kong, Japan and the UK. They are promising new sites for Argentina, Brazil, Chile, Korea and Uruguay in the near future. All can be accessed from the main URL or visited directly. They carry vacancies in all occupational sectors in the US, more limited in the UK, but covering big employers such as British Airways and Tesco. Useful links include a searchable index of news groups that are of interest to jobseekers. These are updated every 24 hours, so vacancies are always current.

Cool Works
```
http://www.coolworks.com
```
One of the most inspiring sites on the Web. Described as a 'labor of love' by its creator Bill Berg, who works from his home in

Yellowstone National Park, the site provides links to details of jobs in 'Great Places'. These include national and state parks, cruise ships to Alaska, ski resorts and ranches (see Figure A.1, Appendix A). Just looking at the site is enough to give you itchy feet! Most of the work is seasonal. Non-US residents generally require a J1 visa (details of this, for UK residents, can be found at the American Embassy site in the visa services section: http://www.usembassy.org.uk/ukvisas.html). Cool Works receives many queries from Europeans interested in these vacancies and plans to build a reference section that covers their questions and concerns. They have previously advertised jobs in European locations and this may expand in the future.

Job Site
http://www.jobsite.co.uk
This site offers a directory of major UK and European recruiters. The vacancies listed are mostly in IT, with some in human resource management. Lists are said to be updated hourly!

The Monster Board
http://www.monster.com and/or
http://www.monster.co.uk
The Monster Board has sites for the UK, US, Canada and Australia. All offer similar facilities, with the language used being adapted to suit local preferences. As well as an extensive current vacancies database, there is a CV/resumé builder that helps you compose an electronic CV using its key words. The personal job search agent, a cute-looking piece of software, scans vacancies matching your key word choices and e-mails you with details (see Figures 4.1. and 4.2). Don't be fooled by its colourful and exuberant appearance. This site has links to some very serious employers.

People Bank
http://www.peoplebank.com
A UK-based employment agency that holds a bank of CVs for employers to search and produce short lists from. Personal details are kept confidential and the initial contact is handled

by the agency. There is an option to complete a personality profile as part of the registration. Registration can be done electronically or via a paper form that is then transferred to its database.

Price Jamieson

http://www.pricejam.co.uk

This agency specializes in new media, marketing and communications recruitment. In addition to dealing with vacancies for experienced personnel, it has a graduate trainee division. Useful careers information is given for all the areas in which it recruits.

Reed

http://www.reed.co.uk

One of the UK's largest employment agencies. It has lots of vacancies, careers information, access to discussion forums and links to hundreds of job sites and careers resources worldwide. It advertises jobs for people from abroad to work in the UK and supports them with links to immigration information and a 'travellers club', which offers a social forum for staff from outside the UK who are working for Reed.

TAPS

http://www.taps.com

A wide range of employers use this agency, including the BBC, British Air Traffic Control, major scientific, IT and large manufacturing companies. When you apply for a job advertised on its database, your previously registered CV is automatically sent to that employer. CV details are kept confidential and can only be looked at by the individual they belong to and TAPS' staff. The site has lots of useful related links and magazine-type features on the labour market.

The following selection of smaller agencies is included as a guide to the diversity of opportunities advertised on the WWW.

Armada Medical Agency Limited

http://www.armada.co.uk

This is an employment agency for doctors based in the United Kingdom, recruiting for National Health Service and private-sector hospital vacancies.

Au pair JobMatch

http://www.aupairs.co.uk

This is a searchable database of families requiring au pairs. Jobseekers can search by the country in which they want to work and the nationality of families. The site can be viewed in English, Swedish, German, Portuguese or French. Opportunities all over the world are available.

Crewseekers International

http://www.crewseekers.co.uk

Crewseekers specializes in finding work for amateur crews for leisure sailing, cruising and racing. There are some wonderful-sounding trips advertising for immediate help. To register with the agency it is necessary to pay a fee.

Digitext

http://www.digitext.co.uk

This is a specialist agency for technical authors.

ELT Job Vacancies

http://www.go-ed.com/jobs/elt-vac.htm

This site gives details of Teaching English as a Foreign Language posts worldwide.

European Crew Search

http://www.eac.co.uk

This site matches pilots and flight engineers with airlines looking for crews on a contract or permanent basis.

Engineering Production Planning Limited

http://www.epp.co.uk

This is a Bristol-based company, with offices in Belgium, Germany, Singapore, the Netherlands and the USA. It specializes in vacancies in aerospace, oil and gas, water, power generation, nuclear engineering, production, defence, communications, chemical processing, civil engineering and manufacturing.

Flourish Recruitment

http://dspace.dial.pipex.com/town/square/fr93

This is an agency dealing with professional catering and hotel staff.

International Guild of Professional Butlers and Private Personnel Limited

http://www.butlersguild.com

The Guild is an association of men and women working in domestic management positions. The site includes information on qualifications and skills needed for a range of work. It contains a selection of surprisingly well-paid vacancies for chauffeurs, caretakers, butlers, handymen and chamber maids. Members have access to a wider range of vacancies and are notified of ones that meet their criteria.

Public Sector Recruitment

http://www.psr-agency.com

This agency specializes in public-sector jobs. These range from care assistants and gardeners to computer engineers and managers.

Thomas Telford Recruitment

http://www.t-telford.co.uk

Thomas Telford Recruitment specializes in UK vacancies for process control, chemical, civil and construction engineers.

Veterinary Locums Worldwide

http://www.vetlocums.com

This site enables vets to look for short-term work in ordinary practices or with wildlife projects or exotic animals. There is an interesting range of possibilities and information on conferences, holidays and publications.

Young Scientist

http://www.young-scientist.co.uk

The agency specializes in laboratory vacancies with UK companies. It has vacancies ranging from school-leaver level to management positions. The emphasis is on jobs that are suitable for those seeking their first appointment.

Professional bodies, academic institutions and publishers

Chartered Institute of Public Finance and Accountancy (CIPFA)

http://www.cipfa.org.uk

At this site you will find details of accountancy training positions and careers information.

Institute of Physics

http://www.iop.org

Here there is a large number of physics-related vacancies in education and research in the UK and worldwide. There are also lots of links to related publications and information.

Library Association

http://www.la-rvs.org.uk

This site contains brief details of all UK library vacancies.

National Information Services and Systems (NISS) Information Gateway

http://www.niss.ac.uk

Comprehensive information on all matters related to higher education in the UK can be found here. The news and current affairs section has vacancy information related to academic jobs and links to a wide range of newspapers and journals.

The Royal Society of Chemistry

http://chemistry.rsc.org/rsc/jobs3.htm

The Society provides an employment advisory and introductory service for members that includes confidential counselling on employment matters and assistance for unemployed members to help them develop a job hunting strategy. The RSC's Younger Chemists Committee publishes a job search guide. The site provides access to a selection of industrial and academic situations vacant, studentships and fellowships from Chemistry in Britain.

Employers

Asda

http://www.asda.co.uk

Asda states that its aim is to 'include a little bit of everything for all sorts of people. Whether you want a recipe or a job, corporate information or complaints, or just to play a game, there should be something for you here.' The site concentrates on graduate recruitment.

BBC

http://www.bbc.co.uk

The World of Jobs pages give details of current vacancies linked to detailed job descriptions, advice on applying and, in most cases, the opportunity to apply online. The advice on applying highlights the need for candidates to research the area they are targeting and show this on their application form. The site contains all the background information necessary for this. Any serious applicant should make it evident that they have made use of this resource.

Boeing

http://www.boeing.com

This is an excellent site for anyone interested in aviation. Lots of jobs at all levels within the company are listed. Online application for them is actively encouraged: 'Boeing prefers that you submit your resumé to us online'. A detailed template for doing this is part of the site. Paper applications are still accepted, but all applications are scanned electronically, so the guidelines given have to be followed exactly. Internships (work experience) for college students at selected institutions in the North West of the USA are offered here. Vacancies are updated hourly.

British Airways

http://www.british-airways.com/inside/employme/
employme.shtml

Vacancies advertised include those for cabin crew, IT posts and sales jobs. There are also details of BA's flight training programme.

Central Intelligence Agency (CIA)

http://www.odci.gov/cia

One of the more unusual government agencies, the CIA advertises jobs you never knew existed. There is a wide range of opportunities, including clandestine services trainees and make-up artists. All vacancies are for US citizens only.

Coopers & Lybrand

http://www.coopers.co.uk

This is the UK's largest business advisory organization and its professional services include accounting and auditing, tax and consulting. The site has extensive careers information, graduate recruitment details, current vacancy information, a cartoon page, access to, and explanation of, the Coopers & Lybrand Ratings of Test Cricketers, links to a wide range of sites, as well as detailed company and financial information.

European Commission

http://www.cec.org.uk

This site advertises the Commission's current vacancies for English-speaking candidates. It has links to similar recruitment sites and agencies in other member states. Job descriptions are fairly short, but there are links to the relevant agencies where more detailed information can be obtained.

Hewlett-Packard

http://www-europe.hp.com/JobPosting

Here there is a huge range of European vacancies that is updated daily. These are not limited to computing, but cover areas such as public relations, marketing, sales and accounts. Online applications and speculative applications are encouraged. The form allows you to select one or more job categories from nine options and to compose a 'desired job profile' where you can describe your specific areas of interest and outline the potential contribution you would make. You can also opt to either state a preference for one of 24 European locations or to be considered for all locations. The company also offers work experience. Students are invited to submit their own project idea as part of their application. The site includes detailed information on the company culture known as the 'HP way'.

IBM

http://www.ibm.com and/or http://www.uk.ibm.com

The US site has company information, employee profiles and links to global recruitment. The UK site has an extensive graduate recruitment section. IBM takes graduates from all degree disciplines. Details of visits to UK universities are included on the site. IBM accepts both paper and electronic applications. The site has a useful list of answers to frequently asked questions.

KPMG

http://www.kpmg.co.uk

Specific vacancies are not advertised, but the site is used to encourage suitable final-year graduates to apply. The company provides a wealth of information about itself and self-assessment-type tools to help applicants decide whether or not they are suitable.

Lego

http://www.lego.com

Take the opportunity to build a digital Lego duck on screen as part of your pre-application research. Current vacancies for senior and IT posts are advertised at this site.

Microsoft

http://www.microsoft.com/jobs

Lots of jobs and information about the company are given at all of its different locations. There is help with creating an electronic resumé that the company keeps for a year, matching it to all its vacant positions.

Montessori Schools

http://www.montessori.co.uk/page24.htm

This is a site where Montessori-trained teachers can search for jobs and post their CVs.

Pfizer

http://www.pfizer.co.uk/recruit/global.htm

Pfizer is one of the world's largest health care companies involved in the development and manufacture of pharmaceuticals. It has a large research establishment in Sandwich, Kent, to which it recruits graduates and postgraduates and details of current vacancies are posted at this web site.

Sainsbury

http://www.j-sainsbury.co.uk/jobs

Details of general recruitment schemes for school- and college-leavers are given here as well as those for graduates. Some current vacancies are also advertised on the site. Sainsbury offers a vacation training scheme and business placement scheme for full-time degree students.

Shell International

http://www.shell.com

Current vacancies are listed here. The site's search engine searches all Shell sites worldwide.

SmithKline Beecham

http://www.sb.com

This is a British and American pharmaceutical company. Its site offers access to both UK and US searches for current vacancies targeting science, engineering, IT and human resources graduates in the UK and US. A salaried industrial placement programme offers experience related to specific areas of academic interest for undergraduates, including those from selected European universities outside the UK.

Tesco

http://www.tesco.co.uk

The site gives general recruitment details and has a frequently asked questions section. It lists current vacancies for IT posts only, but there are plans to extend this as recruitment via the Web has been successful. The company also recruits via Career Mosaic.

—————————— SUMMARY ——————————

- The main sources of vacancy information are unchanged. However, they are made more accessible to all by means of the WWW.
- Searching for vacancies on the Web should be quicker and more effective than by other means. Dedicated search tools make finding appropriate jobs in newspapers and with agencies quick and straightforward.
- There are simple ways of arranging to be notified of suitable vacancies by e-mail.
- Some employers encourage and facilitate speculative applications via their web sites.
- CV databases enable you to make your skills and abilities known to a large audience of potential employers.
- Web-based vacancy searches should enhance, not replace, other means of job hunting.

Applications and Interviews

This chapter examines how sites on the Web can be used to help construct effective applications and gives detailed information on adapting these to make electronic applications.

- Honing your application skills
- Choosing the right method for making an application
- How to construct an effective CV
- Presentation hints
- Matching applications to vacancies
- Interviews
- Sites worth seeing
- Summary

HONING YOUR APPLICATION SKILLS

Current labour market trends mean that an individual is likely to apply for several jobs during their working life. The 'job for life' is no longer a reality for most people – changing jobs or moving into a new career area is. Finding a job to apply for is easy compared to making an effective application for one. Communicating your skills, potential and individuality verbally or in writing can be hard work. Good preparation makes the task manageable, but the act of putting it into words in a convincing way is daunting for most people. Many sell themselves short because they do not know how to word and present CVs, application forms and covering letters.

On the whole, we are brought up to be modest about ourselves, so having to communicate skills and abilities to strangers poses problems for many of us. One man's insecurity is another's business opportunity, and there are numerous ways in which you can part with money in order to get what is advertised as being some magic formula for constructing applications that will secure the job you want.

Getting help with writing your CV

A whole industry has grown up around advising people on how to compose CVs and covering letters. In some cases, help is offered free of charge, in others it is given for a fee. The best sources of free help include university and state careers and employment centres. Such services will not write your CV for you, but will help you construct it by providing detailed information, including worksheets and examples. This information is produced by qualified guidance counsellors, based on research into the preferences and experiences of employers. Fee-charging services usually compose and produce a CV for you. The quality of the finished product can vary from excellent to appalling.

If you choose to pay to have your CV written, check the credentials of those who are doing it. Anyone can set up a web site claiming to offer careers guidance and help with applications. Commercial companies offering a CV-writing service can be found using a directory or search engine.

Writing your own CV

Constructing your own application is a valuable process to go through. If you have real trouble communicating about yourself, you are not going to do well at an interview. It is probably an indication that you are not yet ready to present yourself in a convincing way, and need to spend a little more time and effort on self-analysis, employer research or both. Go back to Chapters 2 and 3!

In the end, anything that is written about you is personal and so should reflect the real you. A CV and covering letter alone do not get you a job, they get you an interview, where you have to live up to the expectations you have created by what you have written. If your CV is slick and polished and you're not, they'll be disappointed! Employers are interested in your communication skills, not the capabilities of a commercial CV-writing company.

There are many places both on and off the Web where you can get excellent practical help on style and format, essential content, employer preferences and other techniques needed to improve your application. All the sites listed at the end of this chapter offer free help. In addition, publicly posted CVs on the WWW give you the opportunity to look at how other people have approached the task and to learn from them. It's often easier to judge the efforts of others than your own!

CHOOSING THE RIGHT METHOD FOR MAKING AN APPLICATION

Vacancies advertised on the Web usually have clear instructions as to which of the methods of application is preferred. Often there is a choice of methods available. Greater choice can mean greater potential for getting it wrong. It's important to follow the instructions provided by the employers about what they find acceptable and what their system best copes with. As vacancies on the Web are accessible all over the world, take note of details about residency requirements. Many large employers, such as the BBC (see Figure 5.1), provide links to their country's immigration departments' web sites. This allows you to check restrictions that may apply. Don't waste your time applying for a job in a country where you will not be able to get a work permit or entry visa.

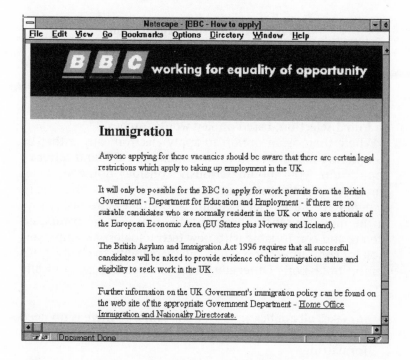

Figure 5.1 The BBC links its application form to immigration information.

CV or application form?

Some employers give you the option of submitting a CV or completing their application form. With a CV, you are in control of what you choose to tell the employer and how you organize and present it. With an application form there are set questions to answer and spaces you have to fill. Some employers' web sites offer considerable help with completing online forms.

An online form should never be completed online, however! Copy and paste it into a word processing package. Work on it with the same care you would lavish on any other application, then copy the details onto the original, print it out and read it again, before finally clicking on the submit button.

Making an electronic application

Developments in IT have been introducing changes into application procedures for some time now. It is common for CVs to be word processed, and employers are increasingly using scanning software. This reads forms 'electronically' and does an initial selection, based on key word searches.

Where there is an option to apply electronically, either by completing an online form or e-mailing a CV and letter of application, you should seriously consider doing it. If an employer is advertising on the Web it means they want someone who uses that medium. Applying electronically says in the most convincing way possible that you are computer-literate and comfortable with new technologies. All employers look for communication skills and adaptability to change; this demonstrates both. Other advantages of applying electronically are:

- it makes all applications look the same, so there is no need to agonize over choice of font, colour of paper or fancy formatting;
- it arrives in pristine condition;
- it is fast and can be sent at any time of the day;
- there are no distractions, such as difficult-to-read hand-writing or unusual signatures;
- when you complete an application form online, it does not allow you to leave blanks as incomplete forms are not accepted for submission – quite useful if you've accidentally forgotten to complete a section!

HOW TO CONSTRUCT AN EFFECTIVE CV

Five minutes after seeing the ideal job is not the best time to start composing your CV. Vacancies have closing dates for applications that are always too soon if you need to start putting your details together from scratch. Your task at this stage should be to tailor the CV you constructed as part of your self-assessment exercises to the demands of this particular vacancy. This means looking at changing the emphasis of certain sections and adapting its appearance and format to suit the way it is to be sent and received.

Writing a CV is not a task that you can do once and forget about; it will need to be constantly changed and adapted. This can most easily be done if you have a strong framework. The basic CV you construct could act as the one you use for registering with employment agencies and placing on CV banks. It will also form the raw material that you use to fill in application forms and produce more targeted CVs. Avoid sending a CV that you feel would do for any employer. Always include something that shows you have researched this particular post and employer thoroughly.

Do some research

The secret of an excellent CV is excellent research – about yourself, the post you are applying for and the employer. The skilled part is using this research to produce something that is concise, coherent and convincing. It is of prime importance that you make it easy for the employer to understand that what you have done or learned in the past will enable you to do their work to a high standard. Just listing your skills and interests is not enough. You need to provide concrete examples of how you have successfully used those skills and state the results you achieved. Clearly show the links between what you have done and what you hope to do, too. Don't leave the employer to jump to conclusions themselves – gently guide them to the ones you want them to make.

Make it relevant

Curriculum vitae literally means the course of your life, but this is just what your CV should not be. It should only contain the parts that are pertinent to this application. It is up to you to intelligently select from, rather than include everything you have ever done. No employer has the time to wade through pages of information. Err on the side of brevity, showing that you can communicate in a concise and effective way and have an ability to select relevant detail. Look critically at every item you select, and if you can't immediately see its relevance to the current objective, discard it. Your CV should arouse the readers' interest, not bore them to death.

Give thought to its appearance and make it accurate

Research into recruitment practices consistently reveals that employers spend very little time initially looking at a CV. Their first glance at it may only be for a few seconds and this short space of time is used to determine whether or not it merits further consideration. The initial appearance is of importance. Thus, the quest for a concise CV should not result in a cramped one. Your font should be easy to read and there should be white space between sections. Reasons employers give for discarding CVs include difficulty in reading them, poor presentation, inappropriate length and poor spelling.

Check spelling, punctuation and grammar by reading printed copies. Don't rely on the computer to do it for you. If you type in 'managed teams of shifty corkers' instead of 'managed team of shift workers', the spell check facility will not pick the error up because your mistaken words are spelt correctly. The possibilities for misrepresenting yourself are unlimited if you do not meticulously check all you have written.

Spell checkers have language options such as English (US) and English (UK). Choose whichever is appropriate to you or the company you are applying to. An easy way to see whether you are using UK or US English spelling is to check a word such as 'color'. If it's highlighted as an error, you have a UK English spell checker; if not, you have a US one.

Grammar checkers will check punctuation and grammar, with similar limitations to spell checkers. They can be set to formal, business or informal English. Use the 'help' function of your word processing package to see what settings are available to you and how to change them.

Think about the format

A generation ago, there was only one type of CV – a chronological one. However, now, different formats can provide better frameworks for presenting some people's details. This applies particularly to applicants with a patchy work history, returners to the labour market or career changers. The characteristics, advantages and disadvantages of chronological, functional, targeted and combination CVs are fully explored and explained in the web sites listed at the end of this chapter. Which format you choose depends not only on your circumstances and employment history, but also on what you feel comfortable with.

Some employers can be suspicious of non-chronological CVs and regard them as trying to hide gaps in employment or study history. Others positively encourage applications that highlight skills gained from a range of experience.

PRESENTATION HINTS

Whichever method of application you use, a basic understanding of what will happen to the words you write is important.

Paper CVs

The traditional paper CV that will not be scanned electronically will be scanned visually. How it looks is important and adds significantly to the first impression you create, so bear in mind the following hints and tips.

- Use paper of a reasonable quality, although heavy coloured paper is often an expensive distraction.
- Be aware that in the first instance your CV will only be glanced at. Consider what the first thing seen is. If it's your name, address, marital status, number of children, driving licence details and qualifications from 20 years ago, it may not inspire the reader to look any further. If it's a concise summary of your skills, it will.

● Make subtle use of formatting tools on word processing programs. Bulleted lists are a good way of avoiding sentences that always start with the word 'I' and can look efficient. Use bold and underline where appropriate. They highlight the text, though, so be selective: if everything is highlighted, nothing stands out.
● Don't overdo borders and shading. A neat and relatively plain CV can have the most impact. This is not the place to show off all you know about word processing.

CVs for electronic scanning

A CV that is initially scanned electronically does not need to be very different from a normal paper one as what is suitable for an optical scanner is often also appealing to the human eye. A CV that is accepted as being worthy of further consideration by an electronic selector will then be looked at by a human one, so has to be attractive to both. Here are some guidelines to help you achieve this end.

● Use white or off white paper printed on one side only.
● Provide a laser-printed or first run typed original if possible. Scanners need clear images.
● Do not fold, staple or attach paper-clips.
● Use a standard 12-point font, such as Courier or Times New Roman.
● Do not use bold, bullets, underlining, italics, special characters, dashes, images, graphics or borders.
● Place your name on its own line, at the top of each separate page.
● Employers frequently stipulate that covering letters and other attachments should not be sent at this stage.
● It is not as important to keep a scannable CV short as it is a normal paper one. The software can easily handle multiple pages and will use all of the information it extracts to determine if your skills match available positions. Remember that it will also be read by a human at a later stage, however.

CVs that are e-mailed

A CV that is e-mailed needs to conform to the capabilities of mail-reading software. If you want to see what your CV looks like as an e-mail, put it in your mail out tray and look at it. Alternatively, send it to yourself! There is no problem with sending an e-mail from your own address to your own address – it's like sending yourself a letter rather than trying to phone yourself. Your mail-reading software may not be the same as the recipient's, but the following guidelines will ensure that its appearance is acceptable on most browsers.

- Send your CV in the main body of the text, not as an attachment.
- If you are composing your CV using a word processing programme, save it as ASCII or plain text, then copy and paste it into the mail composition box. Check its appearance and spacing and edit as necessary.
- Always complete the subject line. If it's in response to an advertised post, then 'application for (title of post and or reference number)' is sufficient. If it's a speculative application, you may have to be more imaginative in order to get the recipient to read it. The subject window only shows around 22 characters, but the full subject line is shown in the title bar and in the main body of the e-mail (see Figure 5.2).
- Most screens show about 20 lines of text. Half of this is often taken up with the e-mail organization window. The first screen may therefore only show a few lines of text. It should be interesting enough to encourage the recipient to go on to the next. As the sender's name and e-mail address always appear at the top of a message, don't fill the first screen with your contact details, put them at the end. Start with a career summary or employment objective instead (see Figure 5.2).
- E-mail screens only allow 65–70 characters (including spaces) to a line. Use the word count facility on your word processing program to check the number of characters (see Figure 5.2).
- Try to give each screen a coherent look. Avoid screen breaks coming in the middle of a sentence. You cannot usually

see where screen breaks will come when you are in the message composition window, so you need to look at it as an e-mail, then make adjustments. Two sides of A4 paper will fill at least six screens.

● You cannot use formatting tools, but can highlight text by using characters such as * = ~ ^ +.

>> *placing text between this combination of characters will cause it to be transmitted italicized by some mail software* <<

As with formatting on word processing programs, use these characters and italics sparingly. Check how the finished document looks by viewing it in your out box or sending it to yourself first.

● If you are sending a covering letter, place this after your CV in the main body of the message.

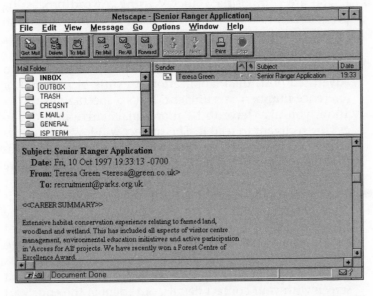

Figure 5.2   An employer's first view of an e-mailed CV will show only a few lines of text. These should persuade them to look further or print it off. The sender's details are automatically included as a header. Viewing it in the out box enables you to see what it will look like before sending it. Note that a full page allows 22 lines to be viewed, and that the first line of the career summary consists of 9 words – a total of 67 characters, including spaces.

MATCHING APPLICATIONS TO VACANCIES

The need to tailor applications to specific vacancies is universally recognized. It is useful to place an employment objective, career or skill summary at the top of the page. This should relate to the job advertised and be in harmony with the aims and ethos of the employer you are contacting. Employee profiles, mission statements and job descriptions are a good way to research this. Where the application is a general one – to an employer or an agency, say – there is still a need to include a career objective and/or skill summary.

Speculative applications

If your application will be held by a company for a period of time and matched against vacancies that arise, you need to be aware of the range of jobs they offer. Your application needs to be constructed in such a way that it will be considered for as many suitable vacancies as possible. Intel is one employer that uses this recruitment practice. Intel's site offers advice on how to prepare effective scannable CVs and includes examples that conform to its guidelines.

Searches are done by keywords and phrases that describe the skills and core course work required for each job. It is important therefore that resumes include terms and familiar industry acronyms for all relevant skills and experience that could be of value in a position at Intel.

A resume should summarize skills in a clear and concise manner. Intel views a resume as a demonstration of an applicant's ability to communicate. It should include all basic information: header, objective, education, key courses/skills, work experience, honors and activities/interests. It should be customized to reflect specific career/job objectives. Recommended length is 1–2 pages. Cover letters should be brief and to the point; details should be included on the resumes.

© 1997 Intel Corporation

Shell also uses its site to encourage applications for a range of jobs. The company recognizes that completing sections of the form that deal with your motivation, values and attitudes is a complicated and demanding task. Help is given by providing background information on issues related to the oil exploration industry and the requirements Shell has of its employees. It invites reflection and comment that is collated by its 'back-packer' to form a coherent application (see Figure 5.3). This can then be printed out and sent to Shell. In addition, the company operates a discussion room that anyone can contribute to and which deals with issues that relate to Shell's global operations. Matters discussed are often controversial, and in many cases critical of the company (see Figure 2.1). Looking at such discussions can help you raise your awareness of issues affecting the company. You may wish to address these in your application, and you would certainly be expected to discuss them at interview.

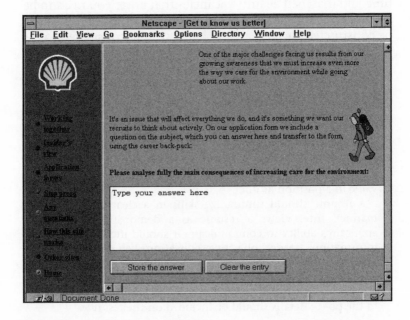

Figure 5.3 Shell International offers an interesting and innovative approach to form filling. It's worth looking at as an aid to constructing applications, even if you're not interested in working for Shell.

Key words

Employers inviting electronic applications generally process them using scanning software that executes key word searches on skills. Key words describe the skills required for each job, and include nouns as well as verbs. Scanning software may look for the names of programming languages and operating systems you are familiar with as well as words such as 'developed', 'initiated', 'managed'. You can usually pick these words up from the job description. The words in bold in the following advertisement, for example, would form the basis for your key word response.

We are looking for someone with a wide range of **teaching** and professional experience in **journalism**, ideally in both **print** and **broadcasting**. They will be required to **lead** a number of units that form part of the **practical work** on the **Media Studies** course. We welcome applications from those who can also teach **desktop publishing** or contribute to the **theoretical units** on the **degree**. There is also an opportunity to develop your own **specialist area of teaching**. You will be expected to contribute to the **development** of the subject at **all levels**, and to the **administrative work** of the Media Studies Subject Group.

Each of the words highlighted is a general description of the skills needed for the job. It would be a mistake to simply repeat them in the application. Use of industry jargon is acceptable in these circumstances – it may, in fact, form part of the key word search. Key words should elaborate and specify. Instead of just saying you are proficient in the use of desktop publishing software, name the packages you have used. It is not enough to say you have extensive teaching, writing or broadcasting experience, name your specialist area, publications and programmes you have contributed to, and list practical skills individually. The employer is using general terms in the advertisement to attract a wide range of applicants, but you need to be more precise to attract the employer. Using key words is equally valuable in applications that are not scanned electronically.

Bank CVs

If you are posting your CV on a database or registering it with an employment agency, you need to be very clear in your own mind about the response you want to attract. If your CV is too general or too specific, you may not get any offers at all. Most CV banks and agencies operate a system where the employer pays to access CV details. These agencies aim to make their databases attractive to employers. This means having a good supply of well-qualified candidates from a range of occupational backgrounds. Consequently, they offer help with the construction and presentation of applications to enable clients to contribute to their success. The help they offer can help you write effective applications for them and others. Some agencies have relatively simple forms for you to complete online, with drop-down menus to aid selection of key skills and other criteria. Others have application forms as complicated and detailed as those of any employer. They decide the format so every CV on their database has the same appearance, only the content differs. Employers will generally perform key word searches to select those they want to look at in detail.

INTERVIEWS

The final hurdle is the interview itself. This can range from an exchange of e-mails to a two-day ordeal including group discussion, tests, presentations and other exercises periodically favoured by personnel managers. Preparation increases your effectiveness and can help minimize stress and nervousness.

The employer is looking to choose the best person from a small number of applicants. Each of these has been judged to have the potential to be successful. The 'best' does not necessarily mean the most qualified. At this stage, employers are looking at motivation, understanding of the company and the post, and compatibility with the existing team.

If you've got this far, you will have done most of the research you need already. It is useful to look again at company press releases and other information close to the interview date. Most company web sites have this facility, even if they are not advertising jobs on their site. The latest issues of the related professional or trade journal are also worth revisiting. This process can help you formulate and answer questions in a way that shows you are informed about the company and the wider issues affecting your occupational area.

In addition, there are sites offering general help with interview preparation. These contain tips, worksheets and, in some cases, interactive exercises that take you through scenarios and offer solutions to tricky questions (see Figure 5.4).

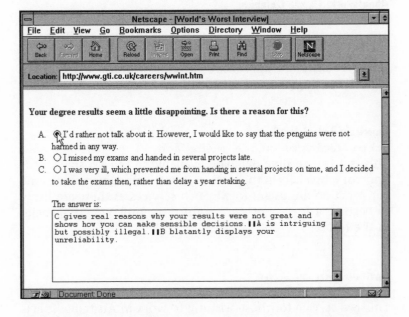

Figure 5.4 The 'world's worst interview' from GTI presents difficult questions and potential answers, then an analysis of the acceptability of each. It also offers the chance to look at the 'world's worst CV' and the 'world's worst covering letter'.

Finally, you do have to come out from behind your computer! You should by now be equipped with the tools and knowledge that will enable you to secure the job you want and continue to develop your career.

SITES WORTH SEEING

Most of the large employment agencies listed in Chapter 5 have CV banks and give detailed information to help with completing applications and preparing for interviews. State employment agencies also offer this service. Guidance sites listed in Chapter 4 offer help with applications and interview preparation. Other useful sites are listed below.

AboutWork: Career Database

http://www.aboutwork.com/resume/index.html
The resumé style quiz helps you choose the type of CV that is best for your situation and links you to the resumé maker. There are three different approaches to choose from: the chronological, the targeted and the functional CV.

America's Talent Bank

http://atb.des.state.mn.us/atb
This is a free resumé database available in ten US states. It is only for jobseekers in those states, but the tips given on resumé construction are useful to all. Such services as these are likely to become a feature of most countries' employment agencies in the future.

Australian Resumé Server

http://www.herenow.com.au
This is a service for those wishing to work in Australia. It acts as a free CV bank for text only versions. It also provides free linking to your CV if you have it posted elsewhere on the Web. For non-Australian residents, a statement regarding intention and eligibility to move to Australia is required. The site also provides a link to the Department of Immigration's site.

Graduate Horizons

http://www.ivision.co.uk

This site gives excellent help with completing application forms, constructing CVs, dealing with interviews, group activities and presentations.

GTI

http://www.gti.co.uk

The 'Just the Job' section has excellent and amusing help with all aspects of making job applications and interviews. Laugh while you learn!

Interbiznet

http://www.interbiznet.com

This site gives you access to a newsletter for jobseekers called *1st Steps In The Hunt*. There is help with CV preparation and a range of hypertext mark-up language (HTML) resumés are available to look at. If you understand the basics of HTML, these can help you see how to construct your own by using the 'view source' command in your browser.

Minnesota Department of Economic Security

http://www.des.state.mn.us

Everything you need to guide you through the application process is here. Samples and worksheets to help you write CVs and covering letters. Detailed comparisons of the advantages and disadvantages of different formats. A practical guide for all jobseekers and all stages of the process. It is part of America's Job Bank (see under Employment agencies in the Sites worth seeing section at the end of Chapter 4 for the address), but the creative job search information is relevant regardless of your country of origin.

Online Career Centre (OCC)
http://www.occ.com/occ
Here you can enter CVs onto the database in plain text or
HTML. There is also a facility for those who do not have Internet
access to send a typed CV that is then entered onto the database
for them. Employers in a range of countries are targeted. This
site also provides general information on application techniques.

The following is a list of employers that have online application
forms and give help with completing them.

BBC
http://www.bbc.co.uk
British Telecom
http://www.bt.com/recruitment
Hewlett-Packard
http://www-europe.hp.com
Intel
http://www.intel.com
Microsoft
http://www.microsoft.com/jobs
Shell
http://www.shell.com

SUMMARY

● Writing your own CV is a valuable exercise. Excellent help with this can be accessed on the Web.

● Electronic application makes all applications look the same and removes many distractions for the writer and the reader.

● New methods of electronic application and selection mean that applications need to be constructed and presented in a way that takes account of how they will be sent, received and processed.

● Interview preparation and research can be done quickly and effectively using employers' web sites and those of organizations producing material on interview techniques.

Appendix A: Getting Started

Time spent familiarizing yourself with the layout and operation of the Web will minimize frustrations and enable you to make full use of it. If you are not familiar with Windows-based programs, a short computer literacy course is advisable before trying to use the Internet. If you can use Windows programs such as Microsoft Word, then navigating the Web should present no problems. The information given in this section assumes basic computer literacy.

- Getting connected
- Internet service providers (ISPs)
- Using browser software
- Navigation aids
- Locating sites and pages
- Search tools
- Offline browsing
- E-mail
- News groups
- Internet relay chat
- File transfer protocol (FTP)

GETTING CONNECTED

To connect to the Internet, you need a computer, a modem and a telephone. The computer needs to have at least 8MB of RAM and 12MB free hard disk space. Most computers bought over the last few years will have this. The service provider you use to set up your connection to the WWW will be able to advise you whether or not your equipment is suitable.

Modems

A modem is the piece of internal or external hardware that connects your computer to the the phone system. If you are buying a modem, the main thing to look for is its speed. The faster your modem and computer are, the quicker you will be able to receive and send data. This minimizes the time spent online, which usually has a cost attached to it. Modem speeds are measured in bits per second (bps). A bit is the basic unit of computer data. The more your modem can cope with each second, the better. Currently, the standard is 33.6kbps, and it will be upgraded to 56kbps in the near future. The best sources of up-to-date information on equipment are articles and advertisements in the many magazines about the WWW. These are available on the Web as well as in paper form (see under Sites worth seeing, Appendix B).

As well as linking you to the Internet, modems can also act as answering and fax machines when linked to your computer. These facilities are independent of the WWW and a valuable extra resource. Check that any modem you're buying has these facilities.

Modem speed

The speed at which modems can work is not matched by the speed at which data are actually transferred; this is often at a twentieth of the modem's capability. It depends on the volume of traffic and the capabilities of all the other computers and modems you are linking to. Like a telephone, a modem can be engaged and therefore prevent you accessing the information you want. A major complaint users have is the length of time it can take to receive data. This can be optimized to a certain extent (see under Cheap Cuts, Appendix B).

Internet technology is changing and improving all the time. The speed of data transmission is likely to increase in the long term, but may slow down in the short term as the systems struggle to cope with the ever-increasing numbers of users. You can always choose not to look at information that is taking too long to get through to you by stopping the transfer and trying again at a less busy time.

INTERNET SERVICE PROVIDERS (ISPS)

Once you have your modem and computer, you need an Internet Service Provider (ISP). This is usually a commercial organization that allows you to access its powerful computers from your smaller one. When you connect to the Internet, your first call is to your ISP, and should only be a local call. The ISP will then connect you to the rest of the world. You pay a fee to your ISP for this service. Fees, services offered, efficiency and customer support vary. Magazines about the Web usually have detailed, up-to-date lists of who's providing what and for how much. They also publish surveys on the relative performance of major providers. Many offer a free trial of their service and that's the best way of finding out if they suit your needs. Whatever you pay the ISP only covers the cost of using its computers – you still have to pay for the telephone call time. 'Unlimited free access' means access to the ISP's computers; any time spent online (connected to the telephone) appears on your telephone bill. For tips on how to choose an ISP, see Appendix B.

Using browser software

When you access the Web, you explore it using a browser. This is point and click software that helps you move around or navigate the Web. Its name describes its function perfectly: it enables you to browse through interconnected documents that can have their origin in any part of the world. These documents, or web pages, make up a web site.

A site can consist of any number of pages and usually has links within it that take you to related pages or sites. Links can be shown as coloured, underlined text or a picture.

Clicking on a link takes you to the new site or page. If you need more information on something you're looking at, a link will often take you straight to it. Job advertisements, for example, often incorporate links to the employer's site.

When you sign up with an ISP, it will provide you with browser software. Some provide it for free, while some charge a one-off set-up fee. Many browsers are combined with other software that provides you with e-mail, file transfer, chat and news group access. The most commonly used ones are Netscape Navigator and Internet Explorer. Once you have an Internet connection you can download the browser software of your choice from the Web (see under Sites worth seeing, Appendix B).

The web pages shown in this book were viewed using Netscape Navigator 3. Other browsers have slightly different icons and commands, but perform the same functions and are similar in appearance. It is not necessary to have the latest browsers, in some cases an older computer may not be powerful enough to run them. Browser software comes with help sections that give detailed explanations of commands. The layout of a web page when viewed through a browser is similar to that of most word-processed documents (see Figure A.1). You move around it using the pointer to click on words, images or the scroll bar. The pointer changes from an arrow to a finger when it is placed over a link. Links are usually coloured, underlined text or an icon. Below the main body of the text is a status bar that keeps you informed of what is happening. It lets you know where clicking on a link will take you to and what the status of the current transmission is. To the right of the main status bar is a progress bar, which fills with colour as a transmission is being made. The mail icon provides a link to your e-mail.

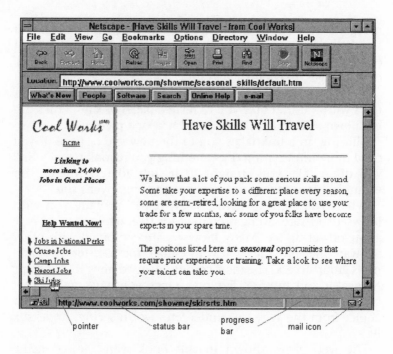

Figure A.1 A text only web page.

NAVIGATION AIDS

You can normally look at browser software such as Netscape Navigator and Internet Explorer without being online because the program has been stored on the computer's hard disk. Spending time offline familiarizing yourself with the layout and functions of your browser costs nothing. In addition, there are certain tasks you can perform, like sorting out bookmarks or composing mail. When you do go online, your time should not be taken up with unnecessary tasks or slowed down by unfamiliarity with the browser's operations. The various commands and menus in the browser program are displayed at the top of each web page (see Figure A.2).

The title bar tells you which page you are looking at. The menu bar enables you to execute a range of functions, such as changing the appearance of your screen, preventing the

title bar   menu bar   tool bar

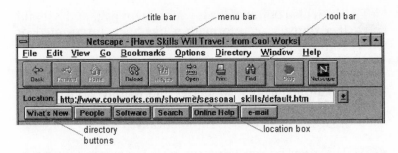

directory
buttons

location box

Figure A.2 Browser commands and menus.

automatic loading of images, entering bookmarks and saving
files. You can explore these functions and alter settings while
offline. Operations such as saving files, copying and pasting
text are carried out in a similar way to many Windows programs. The options section allows you to tailor mail and web
page appearance to suit your preferences. This is where you
will go to access the option to stop images being loaded. Use
the help sections that come with the software to explore these
facilities offline.

The most popular commands from the menu bar make up
the tool bar. Here it is in picture and text form. It can also be
displayed as just pictures or just text. The commands are activ-
ated by a single click of the mouse when the pointer is on them.
When their use is not available to you, the icons are greyed
out. The following are the standard Netscape icons:

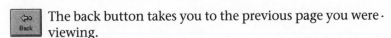

The back button takes you to the previous page you were ·
viewing.

The forward button can only be used after going back,
and takes you to the next open page.

The home button takes you to your home page. This is
the first page you connect to when you access the Web.
It is normally set by the ISP to take you to its site, but
you can change it to a page of your choice, using the
options menu.

The reload button reloads your current page and is useful if a transfer of information has been interrupted or corrupted.

 The images button can be used if you have chosen not to automatically load images and wish to display those on the current page. If it is greyed out, it means that images will be loaded automatically.

 The open button brings up a dialogue box where you can type in the URL you wish to go to (see under Locating sites and pages, page 111).

 The print button prints the current web page. A web page can be any number of screen or paper pages long. The print dialogue box, which appears after you have clicked on this icon, allows you to choose whether to print off specific pages or the whole document.

 The find button opens a dialogue box where you can type in the word or phrase you wish to locate in a document you are viewing. This is a quick way in which to search lengthy documents for the references you want.

 The stop button is useful when transfers are taking too long and you wish to terminate that particular connection. Keep an eye on the status bar at the bottom of the screen to see the progress of transmissions. Your modem has the potential to operate at up to 33.6kbps, but information is sometimes received at less than 1kbps.

The location box gives you the 'address', or URL, of the web page you are viewing (see under Locating sites and pages, page 111).

ISPs provide a line of directory buttons. These are normally below the location box, and link to sites considered useful by your provider. These vary from provider to provider, but generally include links to sites such as:

- 'what's new' – links to new sites and services;
- 'help' – links to help pages;
- 'search' – links to directories and search engines.

They may also include links to software you can download, guided tours of the Web, help with frequently asked questions (FAQs) and links to your e-mail.

All the software has help sections. With some ISPs you have to go online to access the help pages, while with others it is all installed when you first set up your account. If you need to go online to access help pages, don't try to read them while you're connected. Load the pages you want, then look at them offline (see under Off-line browsing, page 116). Print off help pages that deal with topics relevant to your needs and use them to explore the facilities your browser offers without connecting to the Internet. If you're using a public access point, explain what you are doing and ask for free time to do it. As you are accessing the computer's hard disk rather than going online, it should not incur the same charge.

LOCATING SITES AND PAGES

The WWW is made up of a huge number of sites. Each site and each page has its own unique address, known as a uniform resource locator (URL). In order to visit a site, you need to know its URL and enter it in the location box. There are various ways in which you can do this:

- you can type the URL directly into the location box and click on 'enter'
- you can enter URLs into your bookmark file offline, then when you select a bookmark, the URL will automatically be transferred to the location box
- if you arrive at a page or site via a hypertext link, you may not know its URL, but will see it displayed in the location box, so develop a habit of bookmarking any that are useful, then you can access them again easily (when you do this, the URL and title of the web page you are viewing will be added to the end of your bookmark list, then, when you are offline, you can sort your bookmarks into folders for ease of use).

Efficiently organized bookmarks make an enormous difference to effective use of the Web. Time spent doing this is easily repaid later. Details relating to the organization of bookmarks will be in the browser's help pages.

URLs are like telephone numbers in that they only work if you get them exactly right. It is worth taking time to understand what they are made up of and what might be going wrong if you can't connect with the site you want. Getting error messages saying the URL you've just typed in doesn't exist is frustrating and wastes time. The level of accuracy needed extends to whether or not you use upper or lower case letters, where you put your full stops and what sort of slash or dash you use. At its simplest a URL looks something like this:

```
http://www.bbc.co.uk
```

'http://' stands for hypertext transfer protocol. It is always followed by '://' It tells your browser what type of document you want. For normal web documents you do not need to enter it as part of the address as the browser assumes that if you enter nothing, 'http://' should be there. Other commonly used protocols are 'ftp://' and 'news://'.

'www.bbc.' is known as the domain name and tells you the name of the server and company/organization/individual you are connecting to.

'co.' tells you what sort of organization it is. Commonly used ones are:

co.	=	commercial company in the UK;
com.	=	commercial company elsewhere in the world;
ac.	=	academic institution in the UK only; elsewhere this is denoted by 'edu';
gov.	=	governmental organization;
org.	=	other types of organization;
mil.	=	military site;
net.	=	Internet service provider.

'uk' tells you in which country the site originates. Every country has its own code. For example:

fr = France;
is = Iceland;
ie = Ireland;
za = South Africa;
pl = Poland.

American web sites do not normally use a country code. Resist the temptation to put a full stop at the end of a URL – there never is one!

The basic URL will generally take you to the home page of a web site. These are colourful pages that extend a welcome and provide a contents section to help you access all the other information on that site by means of a series of hypertext links.

URLs that extend beyond the country code are the addresses of specific pages or files. They are usually separated from the main body of the URL by a '/' (forward slash). For example, the address http://www.bbc.co.uk/rd/recruit is a series of pages detailing job opportunities in research and development at the BBC, while the address http://www.bbc.co.uk/jobs/jobnow.htm gives you details of the BBC's current vacancies.

Specific files like these can change. If a URL is taking you to a current vacancy, that page may disappear after the closing date for applications for that job and so trying to reach it after that date will result in an error message. If this happens, try going back to the address in the location box and deleting the extra bits – back as far as the country indicator or the first forward slash – and then search again.

Mistakes are often made when URLs are typed or copied and sites move and disappear. It can be frustrating when you've read about a site that answers your questions and then you can't find it. At best, there will be a message in the form of a hypertext link that will take you to the new address. If this is not the case, you should be able to find a site's new location by searching for the site name or the topic it deals with using a search engine or web directory.

SEARCH TOOLS

Unlike other libraries of information, there is no single classification system on the WWW. It would be impossible to make
use of this huge body of information without some index, so
search engines, directories and meta crawlers act as index and
contents pages for information on the Web. They are powerful
tools that can help you find what you want. Many have
enthusiastic-sounding names, such as Yahoo! Yell and Excite,
and they do behave in an enthusiastic manner, quickly fetching
lots of interesting things for you to look at. This can cause
problems, though. You can get hundreds, thousands, even
millions of documents if your search is too general or none if
it's too specific!

The help sections of search engines have guidance on how
to make searches more effective, giving you a range of tools
and tips to help you achieve more precise matches. Searches
only take a few seconds to perform, even if they return a huge
number of matches.

Search engines, which are also called 'spiders' or 'crawlers'
run automatically and visit web sites on the Internet in order
to catalogue them. This means that they are constantly
updating their content. They search by collecting word matches
rather than using contextual information and this results in a
lot of irrelevant documents being included. Advanced searching
techniques can help overcome this. Directories, on the other
hand, are compiled by humans. Sites are submitted by their
authors then assigned to an appropriate category. This means
that they often produce better results than search engines in
relation to the relevance of the matches they suggest, but they
are sometimes less up to date. If you are having difficulty
finding information on a subject, you could try a metacrawler.
These are programs that allow your query to be sent to several
search engines and directories at once (see under Dogpile in
the Sites Worth Seeing section at the end of Appendix B).

Most ISPs provide a link to one of the large search engines
by means of a directory button. Alternatively, you can use one
of your choice by typing in the URL of the engine or directory
you want in the location box.

Selecting search tools

The directory Yahoo is a good place to try out first. It offers links to other engines and directories, so if your Yahoo search is not successful, you can forward your query to any of the other major search engines (see Figure A.3). Matches found are organized so that the most relevant is listed first. The name of the site generally acts as a link to it, but URLs are also given. Search results can be viewed as titles only or in the form of title plus a brief summary or extract.

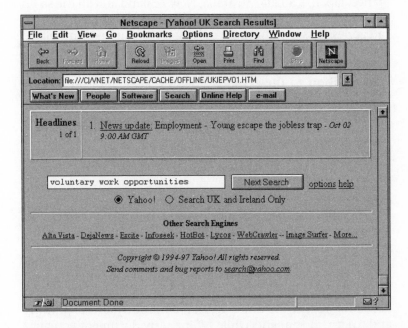

Figure A.3 Yahoo allows you to transfer your search to other search engines, including DejaNews, which searches for news groups relevant to your query. More Yahoos takes you to country-specific searches. This page is being viewed offline, so the file name replaces the URL in the location box (see under Offline browsing, below).

Job and careers guidance sites abound on the Web. You are more likely to be swamped by sites than experience a shortage of places to visit. Try the same query with a few search tools to see how they compare in what they find, how they present those findings and what help they offer in refining or expanding your search. Spend some time familiarizing yourself with the advanced searching techniques using your preferred search engine or directory. Print off the help section provided and experiment with the techniques suggested.

Most search engines offer users the choice of either concentrating on a particular country or searching worldwide. Yahoo!, for example, has specific search engines for the UK, Germany, France, Japan, Canada, Australia, New Zealand and all the states of the US. Most have a 'what's new' section subdivided into categories. It's worth having a quick look in employment-related sections for new employer sites and other sources of vacancy information.

In addition to these search engines, large sites often have their own to help you find your way around and find specific references within the site (see Figure A.4).

OFFLINE BROWSING

The time you spend online usually has a cost attached to it. This could be the cost of telephone calls, provider charges or the value of your own time. Time somehow changes its shape once you become absorbed in what you are doing. You follow links and get interested in what's there, and the ten minutes you'd intended to spend looking something up has transformed itself into three hours.

You can reduce the time you spend online by always printing and reading documents while offline. Any document you view is stored in the computer's memory cache for a time. (The help section of your web browser software will tell you how to regulate the size and content of it and what its limitations are.) You can open these files without being connected to the telephone. They have unappealing names – such as MOP4356.htm – but you can save them as something more meaningful using the 'file' and 'save as' commands. This will save a document, but not any links you follow, unless you save them separately.

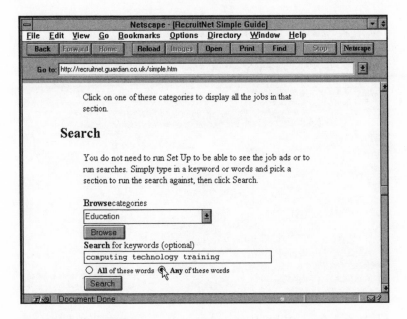

Figure A.4 Entering key words on RecruitNet's internal search engine enables you to make your search more specific. For a general search, it is possible to browse by broad category, while key word searches will narrow down the number of matches found.

Internet Explorer 4 has an offline reading facility, and although this will probably become a feature of most browsers in future, you may need to use extra software to view offline if your current browser does not have this facility. Offline browsers are widely available, and make the process of looking at sites visited without staying connected a lot easier. They process the cache into an index that retains the original file names and URLs, and allows you to follow any links that you made while online (see Figures A.5–7).

They can easily be obtained as freeware or shareware downloaded from the Web. You can find them using a search engine or one of the shareware sites (see under Sites worth seeing, Appendix B). Such software is regularly reviewed in the various Internet-related magazines and comes with various levels of sophistication.

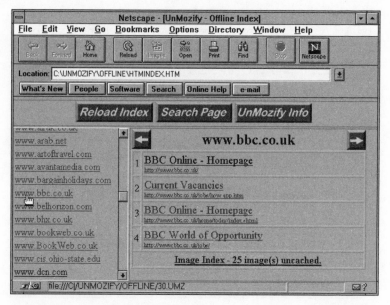

Figure A.5 UnMozify is a shareware program. The left frame is an index of all sites visited, and clicking on a URL in the left frame brings up an index of all the pages visited on that site. These pages appear exactly as if online and retain links previously followed. Clicking on the URL in the right-hand index enables you to go back online and access a live, up-to-date version of that page.

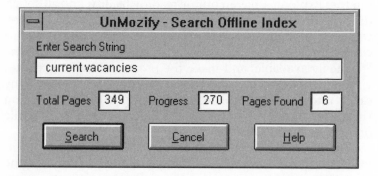

Figure A.6 UnMozify also has the ability to search for a word or phrase in web pages it has indexed. It will then create a new index of those pages.

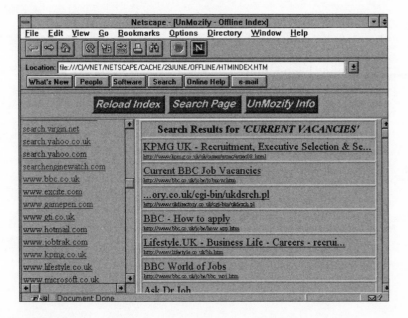

Figure A.7 This is the result of the search shown in Figure A.6. Each of the pages listed here will contain the phrase 'current vacancies'.

E-MAIL

This is the most widely used tool on the Internet. The software for it comes as part of your connection with an ISP, and it is possible to have an e-mail only connection. Everyone with an Internet account can have a personal e-mail address, and there are free e-mail accounts available. E-mail enables you to send messages, files and graphics to anyone else who has an e-mail address. It is easy to send multiple copies of the same message to different people. There is no need to worry about time zones – an e-mail received in the middle of the night doesn't wake anyone. Messages are stored on the ISP's computer in a personal postbox and can be collected at any time. Messages and documents arrive in pristine condition and can be printed off or stored on computer. As the initial connection is to a local number, it's a very cheap and effective way to send things. In most cases, messages can be composed offline, stored and sent together when telephone calls are at the cheap rate. How long they take to transmit depends on their length, but five short messages to five different countries can easily be sent for the cost of one cheap rate unit.

The main disadvantages of e-mail are the same as those of conventional post. Your message may not always get through, either because it was incorrectly addressed or because the recipient chooses not to read it. If it is incorrectly addressed, it is generally returned to the sender with an explanation of the problem. If your recipient chooses not to read it, then there is little you can do. What they see on their screen is your name and the subject matter of your message (see Figure 5.2). It is important to fill in the subject line so that there is some indication of what you are writing about. If your recipient gets a lot of unsolicited mail, then they are likely to ignore messages with no subject line. What you put there has to be interesting enough to make someone want to read further.

Free e-mail providers

If you don't have an Internet account or frequently change providers, there are several companies that offer free e-mail accounts (see under Sites Worth Seeing, Appendix B). The pages you access to use e-mail have advertisements for a range of products and services. Every time you click to look at one of these, the company gets some revenue from the advertiser. These advertisements can be distracting, but are worth putting up with for the benefit of getting a free address that won't change when you change provider. It is normally possible to access your account with a free e-mail provider from any computer with an Internet connection, using a name and password unique to you. The main disadvantage is that you can't compose messages offline as you can with e-mail linked to browser software. You can get round this to a certain extent by composing your message in a word processing package, copying it to the clipboard, then pasting it in while online.

One provider of free e-mail addresses – iName – automatically forwards mail from your free address to any e-mail address you nominate (see Figure A.8). This means you have one e-mail

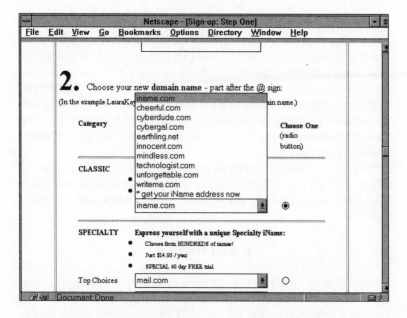

Figure A.8 iName offers a range of memorable domain names. The classic ones shown above are free. Speciality names, such as @2die4.com, @repairman.com, @skibuff.com and @moscowmail.com are available for a fee.

address that will not change, regardless of how many times you change provider. You can use it in conjunction with your browser's e-mail software and therefore carry out most functions offline.

E-mail addresses

These are similar to URLs and require the same accuracy when you are typing them in. Typical addresses look like these:

```
jobweaver@hotmail.com
irene@serviceprovider.net
bill@quackquack.com/
ik@information4u.co.uk
```

The first part is the name you choose for yourself. It may not always be your first name or initials because once a name has been allocated, it cannot be used by anyone else. If the name you want has been taken, you have to use a certain amount of imagination and ingenuity in choosing one to represent you. Some providers allocate numbers rather than names. Your name or number is always followed by an '@', which means 'at'. The next part shows who your account is with and follows the same conventions as URLs.

It is easy to set up different addresses for different purposes. Many ISPs give you the option to set up more than one address and there is no limit to the number of free ones you can use.

E-mail etiquette

E-mail has a certain informal feel about it. When I was researching this book, I sent e-mails starting 'Dear Mr...' and received replies starting 'Hi Irene'. If this happens when you're communicating with prospective employers, you may wonder if it is appropriate to adopt a chatty tone in the formal situation of a job application. Much depends on the type of work you're looking for and what you feel comfortable with. Informality is more acceptable in some situations and in some countries than others. It's always better to err on the side of formality and politeness, even if your respondent adopts a chattier tone than you.

People also seem very accessible when you use this means of communication. The e-mail addresses of world leaders and other famous personalities are advertised and people are encouraged to contact them. (These messages get no further than their PR department, of course, and are treated in the same way as any letter you send to someone rich and famous who you don't actually know.) It is often just as easy to get the e-mail addresses of people in any company you are applying to. However, don't feel that because you can send a message to the president of a country you should also take the same liberty with the Managing Director of a company you really want to work for. Unlike telephone calls, you don't always have to convince a protective secretary to put you through to the right person; if you've got their e-mail address you can sometimes get directly to them. Use this facility wisely and don't alienate people by wasting their time with inappropriate mail. Treat people just as politely as you would using any other means of communication.

NEWS GROUPS

These are discussion groups that you can access on the Web. They are places where people with similar interests exchange views. You access them via software that normally forms part of your Internet connection package. You can find ones that will be of interest to you by using a search tool, such as DejaNews, which searches solely for news groups. There are thousands related to job hunting and careers guidance and many advertise jobs. They can be a useful resource, but are even more unregulated than the Web. To place information on the WWW, you have to go to the trouble, and possibly expense, of setting up a web site, whereas with a news group you simply send it like an e-mail. Guidelines for how to participate and behave are referred to as netiquette. You can find explanations in the help section of your browser software. I have avoided news groups in this book as they tend to be time-consuming and the information they contain is of a personal rather than professional nature. They can, however, be useful as a source of networking contacts, information on industry trends and give you access to vacancies. It is also possible to post your CV to certain news groups. Career Mosaic offers links to job-related news groups and this is a good starting point (see under Sites Worth Seeing, Chapter 4).

INTERNET RELAY CHAT

This is rather like a news group, but it is a live discussion that you can participate in. There are sites offering you the chance to 'talk' to other people about career-related matters. Software to provide access to these, and details of what is available can be obtained from your ISP.

FILE TRANSFER PROTOCOL (FTP)

FTP is used to transfer files between computers. It is called a download if you copy files onto your computer and an upload if you transfer your files to another computer. You won't normally be aware that you're using FTP to download files – it's all taken care of by your browser. Some files you download will have a URL that starts with 'ftp://', while others start with 'http://'.

Some programs you download have to be paid for, but others are shareware or freeware. Shareware means that you get a free evaluation period, then pay to register the program if you decide you like it and want to keep it. Freeware is, as it sounds, completely free.

The first thing you download, though, should be an up-to-date virus checker to prevent other downloads from doing anything nasty to your system. Many files arrive in compressed form to make their transfer faster. You then need software that will 'unzip' them. This is available as freeware.

Appendix B: Using the Web cheaply and effectively

- Accessing the Web without owning a computer
- Internet service provider (ISP) checklist
- Cheap cuts
- Sites worth seeing

ACCESSING THE WEB WITHOUT OWNING A COMPUTER

There is a growing number of places that offer public access to the Internet, sometimes for free. If you don't have your own computer or you don't want to go to the expense of an Internet connection, then you might try the following places.

- **Large libraries.** Many offer Internet access and short courses to get you started. They normally charge per half hour. Although the cost is more than you would pay for the telephone calls, you don't have all the other costs.
- **Primary and secondary schools.** Schools are opening up their computer facilities, which increasingly include Internet access, to the public. This is normally outside school hours and can be linked to free training and child-care. Check with your local education authority for details of such schemes in your area.

- **Universities.** These often have permanent links to the Internet and so extra use does not incur extra cost for them. Many make facilities available to the public and offer short courses to help you get started.
- **Cybercafés.** These are places where you can eat, drink and access the Internet. You'll find them listed in the *Yellow Pages*, usually under the heading Computer Services. *Internet* magazine offers a listing of cybercafés in the UK on their web site (see under ISPs in the Sites worth seeing, at the end of this appendix).
- **Telecottages.** These are centres that offer access to computer facilities and a range of related training. Many are located in more remote areas. A list of telecottages in the UK can be obtained from:

The Telecottage Association
Wren Cottage
Stoneleigh Park
Warwickshire CV8 2RR
Telephone: 01203 696986

- **Job centres/job clubs/careers centres.** All these may offer public access to the Internet for the purpose of jobseeking. In the UK, your Training and Enterprise Council (TEC, or LEC in Scotland) should be able to direct you to suitable local access points.
- **Computer retailers.** Some offer short, free trials, then priced access.
- **Computer literacy schemes.** There are various local and national schemes promoting computer literacy. In the UK, an initiative called *IT For All* offers a free, easy-to-read guide on all aspects of IT, as well as details of courses and computer access points in your locality. Contact them on:

0800 456 567.

- **In the media.** Look out for programmes related to IT in the media. The BBC, for example, runs an annual campaign in the UK called *Computers Don't Bite*. This is a month of coordinated events and programmes. It includes free computer taster sessions all over the country in libraries, colleges, careers centres, shopping centres, buses and pubs.

The free magazine produced to publicize it is an excellent introduction to all aspects of computing.

Advantages of public access

- You don't have to invest in expensive hardware or pay for a subscription with a service provider. If you're an infrequent user, then this is the best way to do it.
- Places with this provision often have someone there who can help you if you get stuck. Some offer short courses to get you started.
- If you're paying by the half hour, it concentrates the mind wonderfully and pushes you into conducting short, focused searches.

Disadvantages of public access

- It's not always available at the times you want. You may need to book in advance.
- It's not very private. Computers are always sited in visible locations so that their use can be supervised to some extent. Web pages are very colourful and tend to draw the eye of anybody passing.
- You will probably not be able to bookmark your own sites.
- You may not be able to browse for free offline. It's worth raising this with whoever is providing access to see if you can arrange to do so for free or for a reduced cost.
- There can be problems regarding receiving personal e-mails. This can be overcome by using a free e-mail address, but with some job applications a dialogue via e-mail may result. This may be difficult if you are using a public access point at infrequent intervals.

INTERNET SERVICE PROVIDER (ISP) CHECKLIST

If you are using your own computer, you will need to select an Internet service provider, ISP. There is a large choice and the level, quality and cost of services vary considerably. Questions to ask include the following.

- Do they have a local point of presence (POP)?
  Most do, and this means that your connection to the Internet is always at local call rates.
- Do they offer a free trial?
  Many companies do. There is no better way of finding out if it suits you than trying it for yourself. One disadvantage in trying out lots of different providers is that every time you change provider, your e-mail address will change. You can get round this problem by either having a permanent free e-mail address once you're able to access the WWW or by using a free e-mail forwarding service (see under Sites worth seeing at the end of this appendix).
- Does the speed of their modems match the speed of yours?
  If not, transfers could be slow.
- What ratio of modems to users do they have?
  If it is high – say, 1:20 – they may be engaged when you try to get through. A ratio of 1:10 is fairly standard. The lower it is, the better.
- How easy are they to contact?
  Despite what some of the publicity says, installation is not always straightforward and you will probably need to ring their helpline at some point. Check helpline opening times and try ringing them at busy periods to see how quickly you get an answer.
- Is the helpline accessed by a freephone number?
  Some ISPs have free numbers for any initial contact, but national or even premium call rate numbers for their help-lines. Several combine this with the expensive practice of answering the telephone promptly, offering you a long list of prerecorded choices, then playing soothing music interspersed with frequent apologies for keeping you waiting. My 'free trial' with one cost a fortune in telephone calls. I even had to listen to a sizeable chunk of *The Four Seasons* to cancel it. To be avoided!
- Can you can e-mail them with queries?
  This facility can be very useful (unless your query is about why your e-mail's not working, of course!). It gives you and them time to think and try out suggestions, and you can

send whole sections of your system files to be looked at in order to sort out problems.

● What is the minimum subscription period?
Some of the prices quoted are based on committing yourself to a whole year's subscription.

● Do you want all the services offered?
Some providers, such as AOL, Compuserve and Line One, are online information providers. They offer extra services accessible only to members, such as weather, traffic and business reports in addition to Internet access. Subscription charges can be higher than those of providers offering just Internet facilities.

● Do they offer free browser software?
Some charge an initial connection/set-up fee to include the browser.

● Do they offer free web space?
You may wish to create your own web page – it's surprisingly easy!

CHEAP CUTS

There are many things you can do to minimize time and money spent on the Internet and to maximize the information you obtained from it.

● Use the free trials that ISPs offer before you decide who to sign up with. There can be a significant difference in the time information transfers take with different ISPs. Different subscription packages are available. Restricted time is always cheaper than unlimited access and worth considering if you know you are likely to just use it for a few hours a month. If, however, you go over the agreed number of hours, the charges per extra hour can be high. Check for one-off connection fees and compare the software offered. Details of free offers can be found in Internet and PC magazines and the computing sections of national papers, such as Thursday's issue of *The Guardian*.

● If you pay for local calls, check whether or not your telephone company has a scheme for offering discounts on frequently called numbers and add the ISP's Internet access number to it. Cable companies may provide telephone services that offer some free local calls.

● Only access the Web during the cheap rate period for telephone calls, and try to do most of your searching at times that are not busy. This varies depending where you live, but essentially it's governed by whether or not the largest user – the USA – is asleep or awake. At busy times, you may fail to make connections and data will be transferred at slower rates.

● Create bookmarks offline so that time online is not spent typing in long URLs. Bookmarks (also known as hotlists and favourite places) can be arranged in folders and moved around. Have the ones you next want to visit at the top of your bookmark file. Explore the facilities available for managing bookmark files offline, using the appropriate browser help section.

● A site's home page is not always the best one to bookmark as your future starting point for revisits. Many are created in such a way that they take a long time to load. Subsequent pages are usually plainer and give you access to the rest of the site. Where access is via a password, it is often possible to bookmark later pages in the site and go straight to them.

● Instruct your browser not to load images, sound, animations and videos. These pages take less time to load. Access to change these settings is through the menu bar and details are in the browser's help section. Some sites allow you to load text only versions from their home page. They're not as pretty, but they have all the same information (see Figure B.1).

Pictures are replaced with the 🖼 symbol. Clicking on an image symbol will reveal the picture it is replacing. All the images for the current page can be loaded by clicking on the images – 🖼 – button in the tool bar. Some web authors tell you what the image will be so you can decide whether or not it's worth loading. In this case, there is a mixture of text and images on the screen, making it usable without images. It is possible, however, to be presented with a full screen of image icons and no text, in which case you need to load the images before you can make use of the site.

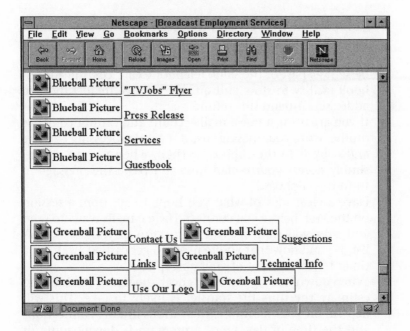

Figure B.1 Here a page is being viewed without images.

- Don't try to read information on screen. Go quickly to any links that interest you – your eye will be drawn to them because they are coloured and underlined. Watch the status bar, which tells you what's happening with your connections and data transfer. Once it says 'document done', or words to that effect, it has cached the link you requested and you can go back to where you started using the back button. Do the same with all the other useful links. (If you hit the back button before it's all loaded, you get a message telling you the transfer has been interrupted. You end up with an incomplete document and will need to reload it.) Use offline browser software to read pages and evaluate their usefulness.
- Print out information gathered in this way, read it at your leisure with a highlighter pen to hand. Mark any links you want to visit and add them to the top of your bookmark file offline, ready for when you next connect.

● Compose all your e-mail messages offline and store them
  in the out tray. No matter how many messages you have
  stored and how diverse their destinations, they will all
  be sent as part of the same telephone call. Use the address
  book facility to store and quickly retrieve frequently used
  addresses. Amend this offline.

● If you are using a free e-mail account and cannot compose
  offline, write your message using a word processing package
  and copy it to the clipboard. Then, when you go online,
  simply access your e-mail host and paste the message in
  from the clipboard.

● Have a clear idea of what you hope to get from a session
  on the Web before you connect. Have e-mails ready to send
  and sites you want to visit at the top of your bookmark
  list. If you know that you're likely to get carried away, set a
  timer to jolt you out of your absorption!

● When downloading software, check the size of the files and
  estimate the time the transfer is likely to take. This will
  depend on your hardware, the various linking connections
  and the time of day. Once a program is downloading, it
  usually runs a clock to show you how long it will take; if
  that's too long, cancel it. If you decide to do a long download, don't go away and leave it; keep checking that data
  are still coming through and that the clock is counting
  down. If something goes wrong, the data transfer can stop,
  but you are still paying for the telephone connection.

● Both telephones and computers are wonderful tools when
  they work properly, and sources of immense frustration
  when they don't. Their complexity means that there will
  inevitably be times when things go wrong. If things aren't
  working properly, it's a good idea to take a break. It may be
  fixed by the time you come back.

Don't assume that the WWW is the best way to research everything. Some pages are only a reproduction of what is available,
sometimes for free, in printed form or as a computer program.
Some careers information sites, for example, may just be showing extracts of programs or publications that are available in
their entirety for no cost at your local careers centre or library.

SITES WORTH SEEING

The following sites are related to topics covered in the appendices. The headings represent key words that can be used to find similar sites or to locate sites that have changed their URLs. The site name can also be used as the search key word.

The WWW

W3
http://www.w3.org
Here you will find up-to-date information on all Web-related matters.

ISPs

Internet magazine
http://www.emap.com/internet
This is just one example of the many publications that deal with this subject. This magazine's web site lists, evaluates and links to all the major UK ISPs. It also has a list of all UK cyber-cafés.

Internet browser software and offline browsers

Netscape Navigator
http://www.netscape.com
Internet Explorer
http://www.microsoft.com/ie
UnMozify
http://www.evolve.co.uk

Shareware and freeware

There are many sites offering shareware and freeware. Examples include:

http://www.shareware.com
http://www.download.com

Free e-mail

Many search tools provide or link to free e-mail. Other providers include:

http://www.iname.com
http://www.hotmail.com
http://www.rocketmail.com
http://www.mailcity.com

Searching the Web: search engines, search directories, metacrawlers

Alta Vista
http://altavista.digital.com
This has the facility to search for documents by the language they are written in, regardless of country of origin. It covers 25 languages, including Estonian, Hebrew and Korean. The sizes of matching files and details of the last update are given in the summary information. There are also sites for Southern Europe (www.altalvista.magallenes.net) and Asia (www.altavista.skali.com.my).

Britannica Internet Guide
http://www.ebig.com
This is a directory that classifies, rates and reviews a large number of web sites. These are judged according to a balance of criteria, including, depth, accuracy, completeness and utility of information. You can search for sites by key word and

'careers' is one it recognizes. The sites listed from this search are largely US ones, but as this free service expands and develops, more UK and European sites should be included. It can include search results from Alta Vista.

Excite Search

http://www.excite.com
One of the biggest search engines, it also offers free e-mail.

HotBot

http://www.hotbot.com
A powerful search engine of a similar size to Excite. It claims to be updated daily and the listings have the date they were written included.

Yahoo

http://www.yahoo.com
A directory based on user submissions. It provides links to all other major search tools and has regional and national sites, such as www.yahoo.co.uk The directory is divided into different categories. For example, education has 'career and employment planning'; 'business and economy' has a 'jobs' section.

UK Directory

http://www.ukdirectory.co.uk
This directory aims to cover all UK sites. It also publishes a quarterly paper version, available free to anyone registering at the site.

Dogpile

http://dogpile.com
This charmingly named metacrawler 'fetches' links for you to look at. It searches web sites and news groups. You can even specify the order in which engines and directories are searched (see Figure B.2).

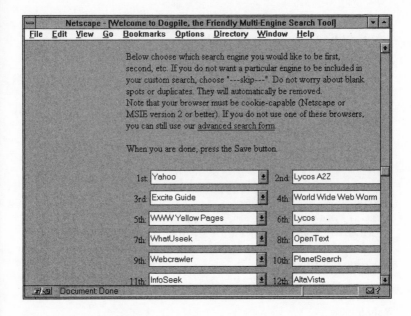

Figure B.2   Dogpile's search engine customizing page.

Who Where

http://www.whowhere.com

This is a directory of over 11 million e-mail addresses. Links to other similar sites and free e-mail addresses are available here.

DejaNews

http://search.dejanews.com

This is a search tool for finding news groups.

The Liszt

http://www.liszt.com

This is a search tool for news groups and mailing lists.

If you want to know more about searching the Web or access tutorials on it, look at www.searchenginewatch.com for a thorough examination of the subject and links to similar sites.

You can register for a free e-mail newsletter to keep you up to date with search engine developments.

URL minders

NetMind Services

http://www.netmind.com/index.html

This is a free service that allows you to register the URLs of web pages that are important to you. It visits your registered pages regularly and reports back to you by e-mail whenever one of them changes. You can also register searches with some search engines. It performs the searches for you and sends you an e-mail when the results of the search change.

Glossary

Bit   Short for 'binary digit', this is the smallest unit of inform-ation stored on a computer. The speed at which a modem transfers data is measured in bits per second (bps).

Bookmark   A stored URL that gives you subsequent access to that site with a single click of the mouse. Other names for this include hotlist and favourite place.

Browser   Point and click software that enables you to view documents on the WWW.

Cache   The cache stores the information downloaded from the Internet on your computer. This enables you to reload quickly on subsequent visits and to look at pages offline

Cybercafé   A café with computers where you can eat, drink and access the Internet. A growing phenomenon.

Download   Transfer of information from a computer on the Internet to your own computer.

E-mail   Short for 'electronic mail'. A system for sending messages and files from one Internet-linked computer to another.

Encryption   Writing messages in coded form to ensure they can only be read by recipients who have the key to that code.

FAQ   This stands for 'frequently asked question'. Web sites and news groups have lists of these to help you make good use of what they offer (and to prevent you from being a nuisance by asking something that's already been asked thousands of times).

Freeware   Software that is completely free.

FTP The letters stand for 'file transfer protocol'. This is a method of transferring files from one computer to another.

Fuzzy logic This is used by some search engines to look for words that are misspelled.

Gateway sites These act as signposts. They contain links to large numbers of other sites on a particular topic.

Hard disk The disk that is part of your computer. This is where most of the information on the computer is stored. Floppy disks are smaller versions of this and can be used to copy and move files between computers.

Hits The total number of visits to a web site.

HTML This stands for 'hyper text mark-up language'. This is the computer language in which web pages are written. You don't need to understand it unless you want to write web pages of your own. To see what it looks like, go to 'view document source' for any web page.

Hypertext link An image or piece of text on a web page that provides a link to another site or document.

Internet A worldwide network of linked computers.

Internet relay chat (IRC) A 'live' discussion on the Internet where users talk by typing messages to each other.

Internet service provider (ISP) An organization that provides you with Internet access.

Lurker A person who reads news or chat group material without joining in.

Metacrawler A program that allows a search to be sent to several search engines and directories.

Modem The device that connects your computer to the telephone network.

Netiquette Internet etiquette. A loose set of 'rules' about how to behave when using the Internet, which particularly applies to news groups.

News group An Internet discussion group. There are groups for every topic imaginable.

Offline browser Software that allows you to view previously accessed web pages and links without connecting to the Internet.

Online When you are connected to the Internet via the telephone network.

Point of presence (POP) The telephone number that connects you to your ISP.

Search engine/directory A facility that acts as an index to the Internet and allows you to search for relevant documents. Engines are compiled by robots, directories by humans.

Shareware Software that can be tried out for free for a limited period. Continued use requires a fee to be paid to the author.

Uniform resource locator (URL) The address of a web site. Every web page has a unique URL.

Virus A virus is designed to disrupt the working of a computer. Viruses can be transferred from one computer to another. It is essential to install software that checks for viruses before you download anything from the Web. If you have a virus, it can also be 'cleaned up' by this software.

Web page A document viewed on the Web. It can be several paper pages long.

Web site A collection of web pages.

World Wide Web The most widely used part of the Internet. It allows publication of and access to documents. Also referred to as WWW, W3 and the Web.

Index